REDEFINING AGING
The Art of Living Alone

*How to Find Joy in Independence,
Live Fearlessly, and Maintain Longevity*

Chrío Zoë

CONTENTS

ACKNOWLEDGEMENT

Writing this book has been a labor and a journey that I couldn't have undertaken without the incredible support and encouragement of many individuals. I am profoundly grateful to all those who have played a part in bringing this project to fruition.

I would like to thank each person who was instrumental in shaping my path to writing this manuscript. My sincerest appreciation goes to the countless friends and family who graciously gave me space and time to make this book become a reality.

First and foremost, I want to express my deepest gratitude to my family whose unwavering belief in me and constant encouragement have been my driving force. Your love and support have sustained me through the challenges of this creative process. I give honor to my late parents, whose unwavering belief has been the catalyst to propel me in this journey. Their constant encouragement and unconditional love have been my strength to pursue this endeavor. I say thank you to my siblings Michael, Anthony, Pauline and Sharon who have now passed on but are the silent voices that ignited me to write this book. Through their life, in their own small contributing way,

I have come to realize that this journey we call life is valuable and how we start the journey does not dictate how we finish it.

I would like to thank all of my mentors and teachers who helped me by sharing their invaluable knowledge base with me, as they guided me from a place of knowing in shaping my ideas and refining my writing. I cherish your warm guidance, encouragement, and belief in me, and my potential and I can attest to the fact that it has been transformative. I am sincerely hoping that this book will serve as a helpful resource and companion guide on my readers' journey toward self-improvement, empowerment, and fulfillment.

I'd also like to thank the team at AIA and Publishing Services for their dedication and hard work in bringing this book to life. Your expertise coaching and guidance in outlining, design, formatting, and marketing have been pivotal in turning my manuscript into a polished publication.

Additionally, I am grateful to my dear friends, who provided much-needed moral support and encouragement during the writing process. I am forever grateful for your influence and for your push to encourage me into what you believe I could be. Thank you all for the guidance and the wisdom you shared with me as I stumbled along my sometimes-rocky road of personal growth and self-discovery. I extend my heartfelt appreciation to my friends and colleagues who provided valuable feedback, engaged in insightful discussions, and cheered me on during moments of doubt. Your enthusiasm has been contagious and uplifting.

Finally, I want to acknowledge my readers—those who will engage with this book. Your curiosity and interest in my ideas fuel my passion for writing, and I hope this book resonates with you in meaningful ways. In writing this book, I've come to realize that the journey is made sweeter by the presence of supportive souls. To all those I've mentioned and to anyone whose name might have been inadvertently omitted, please know that your impact has been immeasurable.

To all of you, your enthusiasm, engagement, and support to me have been more than appreciated. Let me end by saying once again to my readers that I applaud you for buying this book to enhance and empower your personal development. I trust that this book will meet your desire.

With heartfelt thanks,

Chrío Zoë

INTRODUCTION

A large number of elderly individuals worldwide reside in a communal household with their extended relatives. They often opt for this as their primary living arrangement. On the other hand, the living arrangements of older individuals in the United States differ significantly, often involving solitary living or cohabitation with their spouse or partner.

In the United States, about 27% of people who are 60 years of age or older live by themselves. This is higher compared to 16% in the 130 countries and areas that were studied. Less than 5% of elderly individuals in countries within the Asia-Pacific, sub-Saharan Africa, and Middle East-North Africa regions, such as Afghanistan, Mali, and Algeria, choose to reside alone. In the United States, people who are 60 and older are more likely than people in other countries to live with a partner without having young children at home. Nearly half of Americans in this particular age range (46%) live in a household with only one spouse or partner. This is higher than the global average of three in ten people (31%). Very few older adults in sub-Saharan Africa (9%) live in this arrangement. Around the world, it is most common for people who are 60 years of age and older to live with their extended family. This means they live with relatives like grandchildren, nephews, and their adult children's spouses. Almost four out of ten elderly people (38%) live in this kind of living situation, with two-thirds or more in Iraq, Namibia, and India. This is much higher than the 6% of people who are 60 years old or older in the United States (Ausubel, 2020).

While elderly people's living arrangements in the United States are significantly different from those in many other countries, they are comparable to those in other wealthy countries. In general, households are smaller in more successful nations, as indicated by a number of indicators such as education, lifespan, and economic production. People tend to have fewer children and may have them later in life in nations with more developed economies. They are also more likely to survive well past the age at which they are capable of bearing children. For older individuals to afford to stay in their own homes, governments in wealthy nations may also provide financial help or health care benefits. In many European countries, for example, rates of living alone for older people are even higher than they are in the United States. Extended families are more prevalent in developing countries because they make better use of available resources and make it easier to complete household tasks when multiple individuals live in the same home. Additionally, families have a bigger duty to take care of elderly relatives in nations where the government offers fewer retirement benefits or other safety nets for senior citizens. While household living arrangements and economic development are strongly related, cultural and religious considerations may also have an impact (Ausubel, 2020).

As a result, I want to reassure the readers of this book who are 60 years old or older and are single that, despite the fact that your situation might appear uncommon, there are others just like you. Although living alone has its advantages, I am aware that it can also cause a number of negative emotions, including feelings of isolation and extreme loneliness, as well as heightened dread. Those of you who live in gated communities may find it difficult to connect with others in your neighborhood, your larger community, or your apartment complex, especially if you previously relied on your partner or family to do so. To be honest, having financial obligations as an adult might present a number of difficulties; however, managing them on your own can be somewhat intimidating. The management of unforeseen costs, creating a budget on a fixed income, and financial stability planning are a few examples of this. Furthermore, as you get older, you start to worry more than previously about your physical health, which makes you feel more anxious.

You start to consider how to maintain a wholesome diet and regular exercise to suit your particular requirements. In some circumstances, thinking about it can drive you insane. You begin to ponder how to maintain your mental health as well as who would take care of you in the event that you became ill or were injured. Finding a proper living space is a problem as well because you have to take safety precautions into account. You want your house to feel safe and comfortable because these factors can be very stressful. Other thoughts that cross your mind include worry about accidents, the dread of falling, and routine home maintenance. It's not because you're getting older that you can't learn new things, have new interests, or participate in activities. But worry and discontentment might result from a concern about becoming stagnant or losing one's purpose.

These are all normal emotions you experience as you age and live alone; nothing is wrong with you. My goal and intention, however, are to lead you all on a new journey of self-discovery and to give you customized, concrete techniques that take into account every aspect of living alone. I'll put a lot of focus on self-determination, happiness, and confidence throughout my work. Along with offering helpful suggestions and taking a comprehensive approach, there will also be an emphasis on the emotional and psychological elements of living alone. On this path of living alone, it's not just about surviving but also about thriving. I want each of you to read my book and experience a certain amount of happiness and fulfillment as you start your own life. You will also have the tools you need at the end of this book to live boldly and sustain longevity. You'll all have a thorough guide to navigating the benefits and drawbacks of solo living.

CHAPTER 1

ALONE AND FEARLESS

YOU CAN BE ALONE WITHOUT FEELING LONELY

L iving alone does not mean you are alone.

Being social and getting along with others are important components of the human psyche. Denying our innate need to communicate with others and be social might result in mental health disorders like depression. Despite this propensity for social interaction, 27% of Americans aged 60 and above live alone. But there are a number of explanations for why an older adult over 60 might be left alone:

- a personal choice
- passing of a spouse
- divorce
- having no children to share their later years with
- not having any living relatives
- not having any family members who reside nearby

Being lonely is not always the same as being alone. Being alone merely implies that there is no one else present in your space, and you might be fine with it. Living alone as an elderly person has several perks, including:

1. **Maintaining your independence**: Living alone as you age allows you to maintain a much more autonomous way of life. You have access to all of your possessions; you can choose the activities you wish to engage in; you can receive visitors at any time of day; and you can eat what and when you like.

2. **Being more comfortable**: You get to keep your home's conveniences. Living arrangements might change to accommodate the other residents' schedules and reduce living quarters in nursing homes. Staying at home allows you to live life at your own speed and in your own environment. Instead of needing to coordinate with many other inhabitants, you may sleep in or wake up as early as you choose and organize your day according to what you want to accomplish. You can still get all the medical treatment you require while relaxing in your own home. There are several ways to get help if you feel like you could use it around the house. Another option is to have daily assistance. These regular caregivers, often known as "granny nannies," offer a companion to visit for a little additional attention. For home health requirements, these compassionate helpers frequently have medical training. They may help with food preparation, make sure you or a loved one is taking the proper prescriptions at the right times, and even perform some light housework.

3. **Keep in constant contact with your loved ones**: You may invite relatives and friends over at any moment. You probably have a few familiar and reliable neighbors where you now live. There is no doubt that your family is aware of where you reside, and presumably, they are nearby. Even though it is possible, it is a little

more difficult to have guests come and go at your leisure at nursing homes and retirement centers since
they frequently have restricted visiting hours and a
check-in process.

4. **Boost the degree of safety where you are**: You are less
likely to get illnesses and diseases if you live on your
own. As you get older, your immune system deterio-
rates, leaving you more susceptible to catching infec-
tions from the many other people to whom you would
be exposed in a senior community. You may take further precautions to ensure your safety by installing
doorbell cameras so you can see who is at your door
before answering, setting up a medical alert system,
such as a personal response system that you can wear
around your wrist in the event of an accident, etc. (*All
of the benefits of elderly living at home*, 2019)

BUILDING YOUR SELF-CONFIDENCE

Living alone might make you less confident. You can start
to doubt yourself more and find it more difficult to make
decisions. If your self-confidence has dipped since moving out on your own, I want to help you all regain it and
feel more courageous and brave while living alone. The
more confident you grow, the easier it will be for you to
quiet the voice inside that tells you, "I can't do it." You'll
have the ability to detach from your ideas and act in ac-
cordance with your principles. If you've ever had poor
self-esteem, you're certainly familiar with rumination,
which is the propensity to repeatedly think back on anx-
ieties and perceived faults. Excessive rumination might

cause you to isolate yourself from the outside world, and it is associated with both melancholy and anxiety. But by increasing your self-assurance, you will be able to end the cycle of over-analyzing and silence your inner critic (Markway, 2018).

ACTIVITIES FOR AGING ADULTS TO HELP BOOST SELF-ESTEEM

Having self-assurance as you get older will make you happier and reduce some health risks. Activities that are enjoyable and stimulating can reduce cortisol levels in seniors and improve their physical and psychological health. The activities listed below can help older people feel better about themselves.

- **Reading**: As people get older, reading can inspire seniors to desire more by helping them feel better about themselves. Instead of reading gloomy and depressing books, you should read literature that you love. For older folks, self-help books are often a suitable choice. Reading such publications can boost knowledge and decrease stress.

- **Meditating**: You will experience peace after practicing meditation. By meditating, seniors can reduce physical stress and improve their ability to learn new things. The body will be free of bad ideas during meditation, and those negative thoughts will be replaced with pleasant ones that increase consciousness. You may either attend classes in your neighborhood that are appropriate for elderly citizens or meditate at home.

- **Dancing**: Exercise reduces anxiety and supports stress management. To boost your self-esteem, consider engaging in activities like dancing. Dancing improves your mood by increasing the amount of happy endorphins generated in the body. It also helps you feel wonderful on the outside. You could feel happier and more content with your life. Some elderly people might require help when dancing or engaging in other physical activities. It's not a terrible idea to hire a caretaker to help you with this, and doing so will not diminish your humanity.

- **Cooking**: Healthy eating habits might help you feel better about yourself as you age. Healthy meals and snacks that improve your general quality of life are easy to prepare. You could feel more confident in yourself when making meals because you are doing something that is excellent for your health. Make time to cook with friends and/or family a few times every week to make you feel appreciated and cherished. If you require help with this, a caregiver can come over and provide you with what you require. You won't lose your independence because they will only be around you for a set period of time and won't be around all the time; they are only there to assist with certain tasks, so be open to the idea of hiring a caregiver.

- **Setting goals**: Growing older does not equate to giving up on ambitions. During your retirement years, you will have more time to focus on your objectives. You should put in a lot of effort if you want to start a charity organization, a blog on the internet, or learn a new language. Setting goals helps prevent cognitive deterioration, increases self-esteem, and gives you a sense of purpose.

- **Joining social groups**: Having positive individuals around you could offer you something to look forward to each week. You may take advantage of the company of others who share your interests rather than being alone in your house. Consider joining a book club, arts, and crafts collective, bowling league, or neighborhood sports team. Participating in social groups encourages you to open up to new experiences and interactions that boost your self-esteem while also allowing you to discover more about who you are (*6 Self-esteem-boosting activities for aging adults*, 2019).

Guidelines for Better Decision-Making

Making judgments can be challenging at times when you live alone, which can make even the simplest activities challenging. Making important decisions can occasionally seem like an overwhelming or even paralyzing chore. These pointers can assist you in overcoming doubt and moving on with assurance.

1. **Pose the appropriate questions for yourself**: Asking the appropriate questions may be beneficial, whether you're making a decision about a small matter or something that could substantially alter your life. "What am I in the mood for?" is a good question to ask yourself while deciding what to eat for your next meal. But going further might be beneficial for a decision that could have a significant impact on your life. When

trying to make a significant decision, ponder the following questions:

- What choices do I have?
- What are the benefits and drawbacks of each possible outcome?
- How should I respond to each result?
- How will I handle myself if I make a bad choice?
- Will this choice have an effect on my mental health?

2. **Schedule some quiet thinking time**: Connecting with your own innermost thoughts and emotions may be facilitated by taking some time for quiet introspection.

3. **Make a list of advantages and disadvantages**: Writing down your thoughts can additionally assist you in making sense of your alternatives if you're struggling with a decision. You will feel less disorganized in your head by writing down your thoughts. You may choose the one that feels the greatest to you, thanks to the space that has been cleaned up.

4. **Ask for assistance**: You could believe that seeking assistance with a choice is a "cop-out." In actuality, relying on a strong support system may be really helpful when making important decisions. It is okay to solicit feedback and their opinions, but it may become detrimental if you do it frequently out of fear of upsetting them. Ask for people's opinions on the problem rather than what they may do. You could get a fresh perspective on issues you hadn't thought about (Home Care Assistance Roseville, 2022).

KEY TAKEAWAY POINTS

- When you feel happy and confident as an older adult, you are more likely to have a good time during your senior years and be able to take care of yourself without relying on others.

- Independence plays a crucial role in ensuring a satisfactory life for seniors.

- If you struggle with making choices, you are not the only one. Even the most sure and confident individuals can sometimes struggle with making decisions.

- The main thing to remember is that there isn't a perfect option or just one correct option. Every decision we make has both advantages and disadvantages.

- It's important to know that no matter what decision you make, you can handle the outcome, whether it turns out good or bad. There is no perfect plan for making important choices.

CHAPTER 2

THE IMPORTANCE OF AVOIDING SOCIAL ISOLATION AND WAYS TO COMBAT LONELINESS

No man is an island.
—John Dome

The presence of friends and interpersonal connections is vital for people to prosper and lead a satisfactory existence. As time progresses, older individuals tend to spend a greater amount of time in their own company. Being by themselves can make older adults more likely to feel lonely and socially isolated, which can harm their health and overall happiness. Research has found that being alone and lacking social connections increases the chances of developing health issues such as heart disease, depression, and problems with thinking. If you are not feeling well, you might end up spending more time alone and feeling lonely. If you don't have many friends or feel alone, it can harm your body and mind. Having no friends or engaging in social activities can negatively affect the health of adults. Individuals with insufficient support systems tend to have prolonged stays in medical facilities, frequent readmissions, and a higher likelihood of premature death.

SOCIAL ISOLATION AND LONELINESS ARE RELATED

The number of individuals aged 65 and above is on the rise, with a notable portion living by themselves and frequently experiencing feelings of sadness. The COVID pandemic in 2020 created additional difficulties because of health concerns and the requirement to stay physically separated. Being alone and feeling lonely are not the same, but they are connected. Loneliness is a sad feeling when you are by yourself or away from other people. Social isolation means not having many friends or people to talk to. It is when someone doesn't have regular interactions with others. You can be socially or psychologically isolated when living alone, and you can also feel lonely when you're surrounded by people. Age-related changes in health and social relationships—visual, auditory, memory loss, disability, difficulty moving around, and/or the death of relatives and friends—all put older persons at increased risk for social isolation and loneliness. Brain health may also be negatively impacted by social isolation and loneliness. Social isolation and loneliness have been associated with decreased cognitive performance and an increased risk of dementia, particularly Alzheimer's disease. Additionally, a lack of social interaction and spending a lot of time alone may make it more difficult to complete daily duties, including cooking, driving, paying bills, and taking medication.

SOCIAL ISOLATION AFFECTS YOUR PHYSICAL AND MENTAL HEALTH

The likelihood of someone being admitted to the emergency department or a nursing home increases if they are socially isolated or lonely. Additionally, social exclusion and loneliness are linked to greater risks for:

- high blood pressure
- heart disease
- obesity
- weakened immune function

- anxiety

- depression

- cognitive decline

- dementia, including Alzheimer's disease

- early death

Persons who are lonely or socially isolated may engage in unhealthy habits such as smoking, excessive alcohol consumption, and poor sleep, all of which can raise their chance of developing major medical disorders. Loneliness causes emotional suffering in its victims. Losing a sense of belonging and community might alter how someone perceives the world. A person who is always alone may feel intimidated and distrustful of other people. The body's stress reactions can be triggered by both physical and emotional discomfort. Chronic inflammation (the excessive or protracted production of substances that might harm tissues) and lowered immunity (the capacity to fend off disease) can result when this goes on for a long period. This increases your chance of developing chronic illnesses and may make you more susceptible to contracting some contagious illnesses.

How to Stay Connected to Avoid Social Isolation

Here are some more suggestions to keep you connected:

1. Find something you want to do, pick up an old interest, or enroll in a class to learn something new. You could enjoy yourself and meet others who share your interests.

2. Set aside time each day to communicate with loved ones in person, by phone call, text, social media, email, and/or social media. Confide in someone you trust and express your emotions to them. Offer a task that will assist in maintaining and fortifying current connections. Another helpful method for maintaining connections is sending letters or cards.

3. Utilizing resources such as video chat, smart speakers, or even robots can facilitate staying connected with others.

4. If technology is not your strong suit, you have the opportunity to attend a class, either online or in person at your local library or community center, to gain knowledge on email and social media usage.

5. Get to know your neighbors.

6. Find a religious organization that provides opportunities for you to connect with like-minded individuals and engage in practices that enhance your spiritual journey.

7. Investigate the various offerings and initiatives provided by organizations such as social service agencies, community and senior centers, and public libraries in your locality.

8. Take part in community activities by becoming a member of a charitable organization.

1. If you or someone you love has dementia and lives alone, family members, friends, or other caregivers might be able to provide various types of assistance. Seek out a reliable individual, such as a neighbor, who can consistently visit you in person or communicate with you via video call, serving as a person to reach out to during emergency situations.

2. Find out about help and services for your home and community from agencies that help people in need, local organizations that are not businesses, and government agencies that focus on older individuals.

3. Keep in touch with your loved ones using video calls, emails, and social media. If you don't know much about technology, you should ask someone for assistance in order to learn.

4. Chat with people who have similar hobbies or enjoy the same things as you. You can try joining a support group on the internet or in real life. Perhaps there is a memory café in your community that you can go to. It is a safe place where people with memory loss, along with their families and caregivers, can participate in activities and spend time with others (*Loneliness and social isolation: Tips for staying connected*, 2021).

AN IN-DEPTH LOOK INTO FEELINGS OF LONELINESS

Feeling alone emotionally is one thing; being lonely is something totally different. You could want human interaction, but for whatever reason, it does not materialize, leaving you with an empty sense and a need for company. There are strategies you can use to improve your loneliness if you live alone. If nothing is done to combat it, loneliness may result in certain health concerns. Among elderly people, loneliness is a significant issue. More than 30% of people over the age of 45 suffer from loneliness, according to a study. It also revealed that over a quarter of those aged 65 and above are thought to be socially isolated.

Social exclusion results in intense loneliness, which can lead to a number of health issues, including:

- A person who feels isolated from others has a far higher risk of passing away too soon from diseases like diabetes, heart disease, or stroke.

- Depression, suicide, and anxiety are brought on by or made worse by loneliness.

- Persons with heart failure who feel lonely have a four-times higher mortality rate.

- A person's likelihood of developing dementia is around 50% higher if they are socially isolated.

- Sleep disturbances, blood pressure increases, and stress levels can all be caused by loneliness.

- A person's risk of stroke is increased by 32%, and their risk of heart disease is increased by 29% if they are socially isolated, have weak social connections, or are lonely.

- For those over 60, loneliness can be a predictor of functional deterioration and even mortality.

Ways to Combat Loneliness

It's time to modify your situation if you're experiencing loneliness. Try these suggestions for overcoming loneliness and leading a fulfilling life (Brennan, 2021):

1. Consider what causes your loneliness. When you hear a particular song on the radio, does it happen to you? When do you inhale a certain scent? Do you occasionally experience loneliness? Does it depend on the weather? Understanding what is making you feel lonely and addressing it might help you feel less alone. To fill such vacant areas, choose constructive hobbies.

2. Take up a sport or physical endeavor. Did you ride your bike or play golf in the past? You should perhaps try it again. You may recover more quickly if you engage in fun activities that get you moving.

3. Rethink your eating habits. Some meals just make you feel lousy. Sugar is a major offender. When possible, choose natural, fresh meals to improve your health.

4. Play word puzzles, crosswords, or other mental activities. Maintaining mental stimulation as you age is not only beneficial, but it may also help lift the depressing gloom of solitude. Grab a friend, either in person or online, and engage in some friendly competition

or problem-solving. Your mood will soon start to improve.

5. Go for a stroll to burn some calories. Physical activity benefits both the body and the mind. There are other activities you may engage in besides walking, which is an excellent low-impact technique to raise your heart rate and make you sweat a little. You can exercise on your own, with a friend, in a class, or at a gym.

6. Consider getting a pet. Although a dog or cat cannot take the place of a human, they may be excellent companions, especially when you're feeling low.

7. Get some rest. The world appears better after a restful night's sleep. Sleep issues might be brought on by loneliness, which just makes your mood worse. You may fight loneliness and sadness at the same time by learning how to get decent, restful, and sound sleep.

8. Try a novel approach. Consider any hobbies you've always wanted to attempt but haven't yet. Now, try them out for yourself. The opportunities are endless: you might learn a new language, enroll in a wreath-making course, or even try your hand at baking.

9. Interact with others. Find opportunities to interact with others, whether you volunteer, attend senior center events in your region, or take some lessons.

KEY TAKEAWAY POINTS

- Your physical and psychological well-being can be negatively impacted by social isolation and loneliness.

- Social exclusion and loneliness are related, and as a result, both can contribute to major health problems, including depression, obesity, heart problems, etc.

- You should experiment with different methods of staying in touch with friends, family, and members of your community.

- Knowing your neighbors has several advantages, like introducing you to new people and giving you their contact information in case of an emergency.

- Set up times to talk with your family members so that you have a regular schedule and are always in touch.

- Get a pen pal. If you enjoy writing, a pen pal program allows you to communicate with others and develop satisfying relationships.

- Join a new class to learn something new, or pick up a past hobby like dance or art that you enjoyed when you were younger.

- Join humanitarian organizations; volunteering is a highly fulfilling deed that keeps you connected.

- Make an effort to get enough sleep each night since not getting enough sleep might influence your mood and trigger loneliness.

HOME AND SAFETY SECURITY

Your home is your castle; it is meant to be strong and safe. Let's make it secure and welcoming.

Being able to stay in your own home or community as you get older depends on things like your health, how easy it is to get around your home, having people around who can help you, and money. It's crucial for people, couples, and families to carefully think about their own situation and make smart choices about whether to stay in their current home as they get older or think about different housing options, depending on their specific needs and circumstances. When moving to a smaller home or a retirement community, consider the benefits that aging in place can offer. It allows you to remain in the comfort of your own home and maintain your independence. However, moving to a smaller home or retirement community can provide a sense of community and access to additional support and amenities. Ultimately, the decision depends on your personal preferences and needs.

As you get older and change locations, there are a few important things to remember:

1. **Home accessibility**: Can you easily move around inside and leave your home? The architectural layout of many American residences did not take into account the unique needs of the aging population. As you get older, it becomes more important to make sure that you are safe and able to easily reach things or places. Making changes to your home to make it safer and more accessible as you get older is important. These changes can include things like getting rid of things

you can trip and fall over, putting up bars to hold onto, making doorways wider, and adding ramps for easier access. If you are thinking of moving, you should find a house that can accommodate your needs in regards to moving around freely now and in the future.

2. **Social support**: The health effects of social isolation are negative, as we discovered during COVID. Creating and growing your network of family, friends, neighbors, and community resources, including social clubs, senior centers, and religious organizations, is necessary for intentional aging in place. If you intend to relocate, you should also look into the local social assistance systems.

3. **Healthcare access**: Is there easy access to healthcare facilities? Older adults need access to healthcare to stay healthy. Think about how close and easy it is to get to places that provide medical help, like hospitals, clinics, places to recover from illness or injury, and places to get medicine. If you are moving, make sure to look into the healthcare services that are covered by your insurance. This will help you understand if you can still use your current insurance or if you need to get new insurance and find new doctors.

4. **Transportation**: How will you get to the park or store? Some older people have to stop driving for their own safety and the safety of other people. This doesn't mean you have to stop being independent. If you are choosing to stay where you currently live as you get older, or if you decide to move somewhere else, think about whether there are buses or trains you can use to get around. Also, see if your family or friends can give you rides when you need them. It's important to find

a neighborhood where it is easy to walk around safely. Make sure there are stores nearby where you can buy groceries and other things you need. It's also good to have options for getting around, like using ride-sharing services or special transportation services for seniors.

5. **Financial considerations**: Can you afford to treat yourself weekly? It could be something you do impulsively or something you do every week. Take a close look at your financial situation before deciding if you should stay where you are as you get older or move to a different place. Think about things like how much it will cost to change your home, how much you'll have to pay in taxes for the property, how much it will cost to keep up your home, and how your money situation might change, like if you have to pay more for healthcare and long-term care. If you're going to move, make sure you find out how much it will cost to live in the new place. This includes finding out how much it will cost to buy or rent a place to live, how much you have to pay in taxes, and how much it will cost to take care of your home.

6. **Personal health and care needs**: Can someone assist you with everyday tasks if you become physiologically or psychologically unable to do them yourself? It's important to think about both your current and possible future care requirements. According to the government, renewable energy is any form of energy that comes from natural resources that are constantly replenished. This can include solar power, wind power, hydroelectric power, and geothermal energy. These types of energy sources are considered more sustain-

able because they do not deplete or harm the environment as traditional energy sources like coal and oil do. Additionally, renewable energy sources are abundant and can provide a reliable and clean source of power for the future. According to the Department of Health and Human Services, 70% of adults who are 65 years old or older will need help with their daily activities for a long time during their lives. Men usually need help for about 2 years, while women might need it for about 3 years. Purposeful staying at home as you get older might mean needing extra help with everyday tasks like bathing, getting dressed, and preparing meals. If you want to stay where you live as you get older, look into services that deliver meals to you, people who can help maintain your home, healthcare providers, people who can take care of you at home, family members who can help, services for long-term care, and places where seniors can live. It's important to think about what you need now and in the future for your home, social support, healthcare, transportation, finances, and personal health. Also, remember to take care of your emotions when making plans for the future. Think about things like creating a plan for what happens to your belongings after you die, making a plan for your medical preferences in case you can't decide for yourself, and getting insurance to help pay for any long-term care you might need later on (West, 2023).

IMPLEMENTING SAFETY MEASURES

It is really important to make sure you are safe in your own home. Older people often have accidents like falling, getting burned, or being poisoned. Elderly people who live alone tend to be targeted by criminals who specifically prey on older individuals. If you are an older person living alone or taking care of an older person living alone, here is what you should do to stay safe.

1. **Keep emergency numbers handy**: A list of emergency phone numbers should always be kept near each phone in your house. In order for you to read it readily in the case that you are rushing or in a panicked situation, write this information in a size that you can read clearly. Be certain to include numbers for:

    * 911
    * Poison Control
    * A family member or friend in case of an emergency
    * Healthcare provider's office

2. **Take certain precautions to prevent falls**: Talk to your healthcare practitioner about getting a specialized fall risk assessment if you have trouble walking or maintaining your balance or have fallen in the past. Ask your doctor if you should do exercises to prevent yourself from falling. If you have ever fallen down or are afraid of falling down, you might want to consider purchasing a specific alarm that you can wear on your wrist or around your neck. If you ever fall and can't reach your phone, you can press a button that will call for emergency help. Other things to take into consideration:

    * Do not rush to answer your phone. A lot of people trip when they rush to try to answer their phone.

Either have a cordless or cell phone with you or have an answering machine to take your messages.

- When you walk on smooth floors, make sure to wear shoes that won't slip, like slippers with rubber or non-slip soles. Flat shoes with thin soles that fit properly are also a good option.

- If you have a cane or a walker, always use it instead of grabbing onto walls and furniture.

3. **Safety-proof your home**: Make sure all the hallways, stairs, and paths are bright and free from things like books or shoes. Also, practice keeping the entrance-ways clutter-free. Other things to take into consideration:

   - Use the handrails and supports when you go up and down the stairs. Do not place small rugs at the bottom or top of stairs.

   - Tape rugs to the floor so they don't slide around when you walk on them.

4. **Protect your home against fire and fire-related damage**: If there is a fire at your house, do not attempt to extinguish it. Get out and call 911. Make sure you have two different ways to leave your apartment or home. When you are cooking, do not wear clothes that are too big or have long sleeves. Other things to take into consideration:

   - Replace any home devices that have electrical cords that are worn out or broken, as they can start a fire.

- Do not plug a lot of electrical cords into one socket.

- Put a smoke detector in your home and change the battery twice a year.

- Do not smoke in bed or leave lit candles unattended in a room, even if it is for a little while.

- Make sure heaters are at least 3 feet away from anything that can catch fire, like curtains, bedding, or furniture. Ensure that the space heaters are turned off once you have left the room.

- In order to avoid burning yourself, the water heater's thermostat should be set no higher than 120° F.

5. **How to avoid bathroom hazards**: Bathroom hazards are common occurrences for many seniors. Other things to take into consideration are:

   - Install hold bars near the toilet and in the shower to make moving around the space safer and simpler.

   - In the bathtub, place rubber mats to avoid slipping.

   - Look into buying a customized tub chair, bench, or higher toilet seat if you struggle to get in and out of the tub or onto the toilet.

6. **Ways to prevent poisoning in your home**: Never use your stove, oven, or grill as a way to provide heat to your home because they might release carbon monoxide, a fatal gas that cannot be seen or smelled. Ensure that every bedroom has a carbon monoxide detector, and check and change the battery twice a year.

7. **Medication safety**: To avoid combining drugs, always keep them in their original containers. To make your prescriptions easier to read, ask your pharmacist to label them in large letters. Other things to take into consideration:

   • To be able to read the labels, take your drugs in a well-lit environment.

   • To ensure you are taking your medications properly, bring all of your medication bottles with you to your doctor's appointments.

8. **Safety while using cleaning products**: When cleaning, never combine bleach, ammonia, or any other cleaning solutions. Cleaning solvents can combine to produce hazardous fumes.

9. **Protect yourself against criminals and elderly abuse**: Always make sure your windows and doors are closed and locked when you are not at home or sleeping. Also, if you are at home, practice not keeping all the doors and windows unlocked. If you are in the living room, the kitchen door should be locked, as should the door to the living room. Your safety is a top priority. Other things to take into consideration:

   • Get a security system put in place. I am looking into getting a doorbell camera and placing motion sensor lights on the outside of your building, and if there is a dark area in your home, please get lights installed. You can also consider calling a security company to install a panic button system; this will alert authorities in the event that an intruder enters your home.

- Do not allow someone you don't know into your house when you are by yourself.

- Discuss the offers you received from telephone salespeople with a friend or family member.

- Do not give your personal information to strangers who contact you, like your social security number, credit card details, bank information, or account passwords.

- Always make sure to ask for written information whenever someone offers you something, like a prize or a donation to a charity. Take your time to carefully read and understand the information before making any decisions or responding.

- Do not feel pressured to make donations, sign contracts, or purchase items. It's always okay to wait and discuss the plans with a relative or friends (*Tip sheet: home safety tips for older adults*, 2019).

CREATING A COMFORTABLE AND INVITING HOME

Even though I want you all to be on alert and protected, that does not mean that I want your home to be like a military station. I do not want your space to feel rigid and tense, and I am sure none of you want that, either. Comfort and safety can be in sync with each other. Also, how your home is set up can contribute to your mood. You do not want a dreary place that does not have enough lighting, which will contribute to feelings of sadness. In some cases, when the place is smaller, based on how the furniture is arranged, it can make the space feel as if you are suffocating. Therefore, making some changes to how the furniture is arranged and making some practical architectural decisions can ensure that the place where you reside is comfortable and welcoming. Listed below are some great pointers to assist you in creating a secure and enjoyable place for you.

1. **Be mindful of the furniture setup**: Rearrange your living space so that you have a lot of space. Please note that you should seek assistance when doing this to avoid injury. You want your living room to be open with no clutter. Go for small pieces of furniture, like small table stands that are placed beside or near your couch. In doing so, it does not obstruct the feng shui of your space, and you will not have an overly cluttered space.

2. **Go for higher beds and furniture**: Low furniture makes sitting down and getting up difficult. It can cause a strain on your back, among other things, and if you want to hurry to the bathroom, that five-second delay that you experience when you have to get up from that low furniture or bed can be problematic. Higher beds are fundamental for you. It helps with back support, provides huge comfort, and also makes it easier to get out of bed in the mornings or at night. When shopping for a new bed, make sure that your feet can reach the floor when you sit at the edge of the bed. With your furniture, do not select any low furniture, so no low-seating dining tables or chairs that have no form of elevation.

3. **Select slip-resistant floors**: Unfortunately, bathroom falls occur among many seniors. Getting out of the shower with wet feet makes it a risk for you. You should look into installing anti-slip floors to not only minimize accidents but to make the area safer, and this will give you a high level of peace of mind.

4. **Make room for relaxing spots**: Who does not love a chill spot to go and read or take a nap? For those of you who have balconies and porches, don't just leave them plain; turn them into an actual chill spot. Make it where you read a good book or where you have your morning coffee, and for those of you who love the sun, make it a place where you can soak in its rays for a few minutes. Use this area and decorate it with flowers, and choose chairs that have back and arm support. If you do not have an open area like this, you can make a small area in your space comfortable. You can place a small table and chair by the window and make it your lookout spot. Place a flower on the table and imagine being at a small café (Haralalka, 2017).

KEY TAKEAWAY POINTS

- Make sure you can go around your house easily and that it is accessible.

- When relocating, make sure the area you choose offers access to medical services that aren't too distant from your current home. A good support network is nearby, and there are sufficient transit options to get you where you need to go.

- Share your plans with your loved ones, beneficiaries, healthcare providers, elder law attorneys, and financial advisors so they can carry out your healthcare, legal, and financial requests in the event of your incapacitation (West, 2023).

- Implement proper safety measures at your home.

- Keep emergency numbers near.

- Make sure your exits are not blocked in the event of a fire; do not try to put the fire out; your safety matters; exit the building; and call 911.

- Place handrails in the bathroom to assist you in getting in and out of the shower.

- Install rubber mats in the bathtub to avoid slipping.

- Ensure that your home has adequate lighting, and make sure that you practice proper safety measures in your home.

- Do not mix cleaning products.

- Keep medications in separate bottles to avoid mixing.

CHAPTER 4

HEALTHY LIVING

What if the key to aging gracefully is within your control? I am here to let you know that you have the ability to achieve it, and it all starts with how well you look after your body. Your food and drink choices play a significant role in determining your overall health and well-being. Maintaining a healthy diet is of utmost importance to your health, particularly when residing alone. The consumption of nutritious food during our entire lifespan can help us avoid chronic diseases in the long run. It's always possible to make positive changes to support our health and well-being as we get older.

Age-related changes in muscle and bone density, such as osteoporosis, put older people at increased risk for chronic illnesses, including heart disease and cancer. The good news is that this demographic may reduce some of these risks by consuming meals high in nutrients and being active. Compared to younger individuals, older adults often have lower caloric demands but equivalent or even higher nutritional needs. Reduced physical activity, metabolic changes, or age-associated loss of muscle and bone density are frequently to blame for this. Chronic medical disorders, the use of several medications, and modifications in body composition all have an impact on the nutritional demands of elders. Making every mouthful count and adhering to a healthy eating regimen are, therefore, particularly crucial for you all.

Meeting food groups and nutritional guidelines can be made easier for older people with the assistance of friends, family, and medical professionals (DeSilva, 2021):

1. **Consuming enough protein can stop the reduction of lean muscle mass**. But older people, especially those of you 71 years of age and older, frequently consume insufficient amounts of protein. It's crucial to point out that while older people are consuming the recommended amounts of meat, poultry, and eggs, they may not be getting enough protein from other sources, such as dairy, fortified soy products, fish, beans, peas, and lentils. These protein sources also offer extra nutrients, including calcium, vitamin D, vitamin B12, and fiber.

2. **With aging and the use of specific medications, the capacity to absorb vitamin B12 may decline**. Health practitioners can ensure that older people are obtaining adequate vitamin B12 through food, such as morning cereals, by monitoring their intake. You should discuss using dietary supplements to enhance your consumption of vitamin B12 with your healthcare professionals.

HEALTHY DRINK OPTIONS FOR SENIORS

Because the ability to feel thirsty decreases with age, it can be challenging for older people to consume enough liquids to stay hydrated. Water doesn't have any calories, so drinking plenty of it is a fantastic method to aid digestion and avoid being dehydrated. Also, consider fruit juices that haven't been sweetened, low-fat or fat-free milk, and fortified soy drinks, which can also aid in supplying fluid and nutritional requirements. You might be reminded by healthcare professionals, family members, and/or friends to drink water with meals and throughout the day. A reminder system for drinking water might also be considered and placed all over your home. If you decide to drink, you should only do so in moderation. Males should limit their intake to two drinks per day, while women should limit their intake to one. As you age, keep in mind that the effects of alcohol hit you more rapidly than they did when you were younger. This might lead to an increased risk of mishaps, such as falls.

ENCOURAGEMENT OF HEALTHY EATING AMONG OLDER ADULTS

Similar to earlier life phases, family, friends, and health experts may assist older people in maintaining a balanced eating pattern that suits their spending limits, food choices, and cultural customs. When encouraging older persons to eat healthfully, other aspects to take into account include (DeSilva, 2021):

- **Appreciation of food**: In addition to changing your eating habits, dining with friends and family may boost food satisfaction and offer a wonderful opportunity to share life's experiences.

- **The capacity to swallow or chew food**: You can find textures that are agreeable, attractive, and delightful for you by experimenting with various cooking methods for meals from all food categories, especially if you have trouble chewing or swallowing. Having healthy teeth is essential for being able to chew food.

- **Food sustainability**: Elderly people should focus on practicing safe food handling. With advancing years, immune system performance declines, increasing the probability of foodborne illness.

The Importance of Meal Planning

Hey, let me not mince my words here; solo cooking can be a tough task. Nevertheless, I can guide you through the steps to ensure it becomes an easy task (Ball, 2022):

1. **Make a plan**: Creating a weekly menu plan and a grocery list is a beneficial step to take if you haven't done so yet. When you plan your menu, you remove any uncertainty and know exactly what ingredients you need for meals during the week. After making a plan, check what things you already have and what things you need to buy from the store. This will make your grocery shopping easier and help you save money by not buying unnecessary or unused items. Bonus: It also helps you reduce the amount of food you waste.

2. **Cut the recipes in half and use any extra food from previous meals**: Living alone can be difficult when it comes to cooking because most recipes are made to serve a larger number of people, usually four or six. Instead of having too much leftover food, you can solve this by learning to make smaller portions of recipes. You can halve the recipe or even divide it by three if it's meant for six people. This lets you choose how much food you want to make.

3. **Switch to a plant-based diet**: These days, a lot of us don't have much money, and meat costs a lot. Eating

more plant-based food can actually help you save a lot of money. Not only are vegan and vegetarian protein sources, such as beans and legumes, very cheap, but they also have a lot of healthy substances.

4. **Make use of your freezer**: You can also put perishable foods like bread in the freezer. It can be challenging for one person to consume a whole loaf of bread before it goes bad. Just cut, put in the freezer, and take out a few slices when you want them. Having a lot of food in your freezer can help you quickly make healthy meals. Additionally, you have the option to store extra food in the freezer for a future day when you are unable to prepare a meal due to a lack of time or energy.

Tailoring Exercise to Fit Your Individual Needs

In conjunction with maintaining a nutritious eating habit, staying active is essential. Engaging in physical activity benefits both your physical and mental well-being. Maintaining an active lifestyle while living alone has the potential to enhance your well-being and ensure good physical condition. It aids in extending your lifespan. Engaging in a moderate level of physical activity can contribute to enhancing the general well-being of elderly individuals. You can mix activities like walking and aerobics with strength-training exercises. If you're an older adult wanting to start exercising regularly, you should aim to do 150 minutes of moderate exercise each week. You can do activities like walking, swimming, or cycling every day to help make your body stronger, more flexible, and more balanced. Persons over the age of 65 who maintain good health and physical fitness are recommended by the

Centers for Disease Control and Prevention to follow this timeframe. Even though it may seem like a lot, the good news is that you can divide it into smaller chunks of exercise that only take 10 or 15 minutes. You can do these smaller exercises two or more times a day (Kilroy, 2022).

It's also crucial to consult your healthcare professional before beginning a particular activity. They can also advise you on the most suitable kind of exercise for your needs. It's critical that you select workouts that are appropriate for your physical makeup and degree of strength. Injuries and fatalities among older people in North America are most frequently brought on by falls. You do not have to become a victim of slips and falls, though. You may strengthen and balance yourself through exercise, allowing you to walk taller and with greater confidence.

For seniors who want to enhance their balance, I've provided several exercises below (*14 exercises for seniors to improve strength and balance*, 2023):

1. **Single-limb stance**: For older citizens, it's preferable to begin with a straightforward balancing exercise. How to do it: Hold on to the back of a stable, sturdy chair (not one with wheels) as you stand behind it. Raise your right foot so you can stand on your left. As long as you can, maintain that stance; then, alternate your feet. The objective is to stand on one foot without grabbing the chair and maintain that position for up to a minute.

2. **Back leg raises**: With this senior strength exercise, you strengthen your lower back and your glutes. Step

back from a chair. Do not point your toes or bend your knees as you slowly raise your right leg straight back. Hold that position for a moment, then gradually drop your leg. Ten to fifteen times for each leg.

3. **Single-limb stance with arm**: Your physical coordination will be improved by this balance exercise. Standing with your feet together and your arms by your sides, close to a chair. Over your head, raise your left hand. After that, gradually lift your left foot off the ground. For 10 seconds, maintain that posture. On the right side, carry out the same process.

4. **Side leg raise**: For this balance-enhancing workout, you'll need a chair. Your feet should be slightly apart as you stand behind the chair. Lift your right leg slowly to the side. Your toe should be pointed forward while you maintain a straight posture. Slowly lower your right leg. Repeat this exercise 10–15 times for each leg.

5. **Marching in place**: Seniors can improve their balance by marching. Perform this exercise while in front of a counter if you require a handhold. Lift as high as you can with your right knee while standing straight. After lowering it, raise the left leg. Legs were raised and lowered 20 times.

6. **Shoulder rolls**: Rotate your shoulders slowly upward to the ceiling, then downward. Then, repeat the process, rolling the objects downward after rolling them forward. It is important to note that this exercise can be done seated or standing.

EXERCISE AND YOUR MENTAL WELL-BEING

Exercise plays a crucial role in improving your health and overall emotional well-being, transcending its impacts solely on the body. As previously mentioned, living in solitude can evoke feelings of loneliness and sadness, and my intention is for none of you who live alone to experience such emotions. It is essential for solitary older individuals to proactively safeguard against experiencing depression. Depression can have a negative impact on your mental state and can sometimes cause you to distance yourself from loved ones. Regularly participating in exercise has the potential to significantly ease feelings of depression and anxiety. It also helps you relax, remember things better, sleep well, and make you feel happier overall. You don't need to be obsessed with fitness to enjoy the advantages. Studies show that even small amounts of exercise can have a positive impact. Irrespective of age or level of physical fitness, anyone can acquire the ability to utilize exercise for improving mental health, boosting energy levels, enhancing emotional well-being, and leading a more satisfying existence. Exercise helps boost your mood and fight against depression for many different reasons. This is highly significant as it encourages brain growth, reduces inflammation, and fosters the development of beneficial neural networks, resulting in a sense of tranquility and well-being. It also makes your brain release chemicals called endorphins that boost your mood and make you feel happy. Exercise has the potential to redirect your focus away from negative thoughts and offer a peaceful escape from depression.

OTHER MENTAL HEALTH BENEFITS OF EXERCISE

Even if you don't have a mental health issue, exercising regularly can still improve your mood, perspective, and overall mental health. Engaging in exercise is crucial for maintaining overall well-being (Robinson, 2023):

1. **Enhanced memory and improved cognitive abilities**: The neurotransmitters responsible for generating feelings of happiness are also beneficial for enhancing focus and cognitive abilities. Physical activity also encourages the development of new brain cells and can slow down the decline that comes with aging.

2. **Increase in self-esteem**: Doing regular activities is like investing in yourself. It helps you take care of your thoughts, physical health, and inner being. When something becomes a regular thing you do, it can help you feel good about yourself and make you feel confident and strong. You will feel more confident about how you look, and by reaching even small exercise targets, you will feel proud of yourself.

3. **Sleeping more soundly**: Doing a little bit of exercise in the morning or afternoon can help control your sleep schedule. If you enjoy exercising before going to sleep, incorporating calming exercises like yoga or stretching can enhance your sleep experience.

4. **Additional power or strength**: Exercising to make your heartbeat faster a few times each week will help you feel more energized. Begin with a small amount of

exercise each day, and gradually do more as you start to feel more energetic.

5. **Being able to bounce back and recover quickly from difficult situations or setbacks**: When you face difficult mental or emotional problems, exercising can help you become stronger and handle them in a healthy way. It is better to choose exercise instead of turning to alcohol, drugs, or other harmful actions that will only make your symptoms worse. Exercise regularly can make your immune system stronger and decrease the negative effects of stress.

KEY TAKEAWAY POINTS

- One of the best things about meal prep is that it lets you plan and prepare just the right amount of food for each serving.

- Planning your meals in advance can help you save money.

- Planning your meals in advance helps you make healthier food choices because it prevents you from making impulsive decisions when you are hungry. Making impulsive choices about what to eat often results in consuming unhealthy food.

- With pre-prepared meals, you will always have home-made food that is already cooked and can be easily reheated and eaten.

- Being active is good for you in multiple ways. Not only does it contribute to physical well-being, but it also bolsters your mental and emotional state. It helps you feel calm and worry-free.

- Consider physical activity as part of your everyday routine instead of viewing it as a task to complete. Take a look at your daily schedule and think about ways to fit in and exercise in different places throughout the day.

- Transition from the interior to the exterior of your residence. Clean the house, take care of the yard and garden, and use a broom to sweep the sidewalk or patio.

- Get moving and have fun with your family, friends, and/or people who live near you. Make riding bikes around your neighborhood with your kids and grand-kids a regular part of your weekends. Spend time gardening with your family and friends. Go canoeing at a nearby lake. If you have a dog, take your dog for a walk around the neighborhood. If your community has a group of people who like to walk together, it would be a good idea for you to join them. Or if they do exercise activities in the park, you should register to take part as well.

CHAPTER 5

FINANCIAL INDEPENDENCE

An astonishing statistic reveals that 80% (47 million) of people who are 60 years of age or older do not possess sufficient financial resources to manage long-term care expenses or other financial hardships. Unfortunately, there are many people who fail to begin preparing for their elderly years until it becomes too late or, in some cases, mishandle their saved finances (*80% of older Americans cannot pay for long-term care or withstand a financial shock, new study shows*, 2023).

The most important thing to do is make a plan for how you will spend your money. I must stress that it is important to always have a plan. Some common costs for retired people to consider are paying for a place to live, medical care, food, and getting around. Making a retirement budget is a straightforward process of collecting and examining all your necessary and extra expenses and then comparing them with how much money you have coming in. Thinking carefully and being organized can help reduce stress and help you achieve your retirement goals. Planning your finances for retirement is like planning your finances at any other time in life. The process is the same, but where the money comes from and how it is used are different. For instance, you may not be receiving a salary anymore, but you are likely receiving money from Social Security and withdrawing funds from your retirement savings, such as a 401(k), IRA, annuity, or other savings plans.

Here are some guidelines for things you should always consider when making a budget:

- assemble all financial documentation.

- identify your variable and fixed costs.

- sort your costs into necessary and unnecessary categories.

- make a list of your one-time costs.

- determine all sources of retirement income, such as Social Security, disbursements from retirement accounts, and annuity payments.

- calculate the proportion of necessary to optional spending.

- compared to your income, compare these costs.

- assess if you need to change your spending habits.

- think about your personal objectives and desired retirement lifestyle, then alter as necessary.

For those of you without sufficient funds, a budget that is achievable is essential. Start by creating a detailed picture of your projected retirement income. This phase is essential to creating a trustworthy retirement budget because it most likely won't represent your pre-retirement income. Consider all elements that might have an impact on your revenue, such as:

- inflation

- rate of interest on savings and investment accounts

- recurring payments

- payments from pensions

- date of retirement

- retirement age

- taxes

- passive sources of income, such as rent from a rental property or book royalties

- income from a contract, consultancy, or part-time job

- social security advantages

Once you have a decent sense of how much money will come in each month, take your requirements and aspirations for your lifestyle into account. Consider the following inquiries for yourself:

- What do I hope to accomplish during my golden years?

- What aspects of my existing way of life won't I alter or give up?

- How much financial assistance will I give to my kids and grandkids?

- What sort of inheritance am I hoping to leave?

- Is maintaining my existing residence vital to me?

- How can I deal with being alone on a mental and emotional level?

SHOCKS AND OTHER CONSIDERATIONS

In your retirement years, experiencing unexpected financial difficulties can also affect your mental and emotional well-being. Making decisions can be hard when something sudden and upsetting happens, like the death of a husband or wife, getting divorced, becoming disabled, or needing sudden home repairs. These things impact you in many ways and can make you feel overwhelmed, and that is a normal feeling to experience. That is why having money saved up for situations like this can help not just with your financial situation but also with your emotions and how you feel overall. Budgeting for unexpected situations means setting aside money for unexpected expenses. It is similar to having an emergency fund, in which financial experts recommend having enough money to cover three months' worth of salary for people who work. Researchers have found that over two-thirds of adults who are 70 years of age or older go through at least one bad experience within a span of nine years (Borwick, 2023).

Common problems experienced by retirees include:

- home upkeep and repairs, this can be truly trying.
- significant dental costs
- unusually high medical costs
- widowhood
- divorce
- investing pitfalls

SMART INVESTING FOR A SOLO FUTURE

A lot of people get concerned about how much money they have saved for retirement when they reach their 50s, and retirement is getting closer. If you haven't saved enough yet, please do not stress about it. Take that first step and just make a plan to save the amount you need. Providing essential guidance, I will provide information for individuals aged fifty and above on strategies to save and invest money for their retirement. Another option to consider is to get assistance from a financial advisor who knows a lot about planning for retirement. This is a great idea to look into. Now is the time to start being serious about your finances so that you are prepared for your later years. There is no strict rule for how much money you should have saved by the time you reach fifty, but there are average amounts that can help you estimate if you are lagging behind. In simple words, experts believe that having five to six times your yearly salary saved is a good goal for retirement. However, the amount you need also depends on your future plans after retiring. You can't change what happened in the past, so don't worry about what you should have done. Instead, focus on what you can do now to prepare for retirement. You can still begin saving for retirement even if you are fifty years old and have not saved any money yet.

Here are the things you can do and the choices you have:

1. Start a retirement account. Trust me, this is a great way to get started. You need to use a retirement savings account to invest your money. Having a way to save money, like a retirement account, is important to all of you. It could be a 401(k), 403(b), traditional IRA, Roth IRA, or another type of plan. If you are saving a lot of money by the time you are fifty, it likely means that you are getting close to retiring. Because of this, some experts suggest picking safer investment options, such as bonds. You may not make a lot of money as you would with stocks, but you also won't lose a lot

even if the market becomes uncertain. The last thing any of you want to do is lose.

2. Make the most of your catch-up contributions. One more thing to keep in mind is that now that you're over fifty, you can contribute more money to your 401(k) retirement account. In 2023, workers can usually put $22,500 each year towards their retirement savings. If you are over fifty years old, you have the option to add an extra $7,500 to your contributions because of the catch-up contribution limits available to you now. Suppose you are able to. Try to contribute the maximum amount to your 401(k) plan. Make sure to check if your company will add money to your 401(k) savings. This is like getting extra money for your retirement savings, so try to put in the same amount as your employer does. Additionally, make sure to understand the rules about 401(k) vesting: Some companies might need you to work for a specific period before the matching funds from the company become fully yours.

3. Think about starting your own business. I know some of you might read this and think that this makes no sense as you are now in your fifties. However, by the time you reach your fifties, it is highly probable that you have accumulated an extensive amount of expertise in whatever field you worked in and your overall professional experience. If you begin saving money for the future later in life, it may not be so bad if you can start a business that does well. This is usually the best way to make the most money if it works out. If you work for yourself, you can save for retirement and receive extra money from your business.

I want you all to keep in mind that taxes continue to be mandatory even if you're not working anymore. When you think about your retirement, remember to consider the taxes you will have to pay. If you have saved money for retirement using a traditional 401(k) or IRA, you will need to pay taxes on that money when you receive it during your retirement (Geier, 2023).

KEY TAKEAWAY POINTS

- Around 20% of older homes, which is approximately 11 million, lack any support system for aging individuals.

- More than five years of care will be required for one in every seven older adults.

- It could be beneficial to seek assistance from a financial advisor in managing your finances. A finance expert will use their knowledge to assist you in achieving your retirement objectives.

CHAPTER
"GOOD WILL"

Helping others without expectation of anything in return has been proven to lead to increased happiness and satisfaction in life.

I would love to give you the chance to experience that same feeling during your reading or listening experience today...

All it takes is a few moments of your time to answer one simple question:

Would you make a difference in the life of someone you've never met—without spending any money or seeking recognition for your good will?

If so, I have a small request for you.

If you've found value in your reading or listening experience today, I humbly ask that you take a brief moment right now to leave an honest review of this book. It won't cost you anything but 30 seconds of your time—just a few seconds to share your thoughts with others.

Your voice can go a long way in helping someone else find the same inspiration and knowledge that you have.

Are you familiar with leaving a review for an Audible, Kindle, or e-reader book? If so, it's simple:

If you're on **Audible**: just hit the three dots in the top right of your device, click rate & review, then leave a few sentences about the book along with your star rating.

If you're reading on **Kindle** or an e-reader, simply scroll to the last page of the book and swipe up—the review should prompt from there.

If you're on a **Paperback** or any other physical format of this book, you can find the book page on Amazon (or wherever you bought this) and leave your review right there.

CHAPTER 6

CONTINUOUS GROWTH

Many people oftentimes feel that once they have reached a certain age, they can no longer pursue certain dreams or that there is no chance of achieving any real success. This way of thinking stems from what they were taught early in their development. In fact, many of us were told that we had to accomplish certain things by a particular age, or it would never be possible. This is what causes many people to feel unaccomplished in their late twenties or early thirties if they are not married with children or homeowners or do not have flourishing careers. Having that mindset that if you have not done certain things by a certain age, it can almost make you stagnant and make you feel like a failure when you are not. It also causes high levels of anxiety and can feed depression. I want you all to know that there is no one method that works for everyone. We are all different people; we all have different methods of learning, etc. We all face various trials and circumstances that delay certain things from happening at particular times. It does not mean something is wrong with you; it just means that things will occur for you later on in your life. Fast forward to being an elder, and some of you are more than likely starting to feel that you are too old to start a business and achieve true success or that any other accomplishments or dreams that you had when you were younger are not achievable. If any of you believe or think this, I want you to dismiss it from your mind. You are capable of greatness at any age in life; your age does not define you.

You can achieve success over fifty; your life is not over, and you are not too old! To be frank with you, you can change your life at any age. However, it is a process and will not happen overnight. You will need to be patient with yourself. With preparation and mindfulness, you can make immense and remarkable changes in your life. Your mind is limitless; you can always develop, learn, and improve yourself. Never stop learning and wanting to evolve. At each stage in your growth as a human, life will always provide a way to self-improve and progress.

Because I want you all to feel motivated and really embrace who you are, listed below are several people who managed to achieve success over fifty (*Success over 50: Top 10 career success stories*, 2021):

1. **Harry Bernstein**: Published writer at 96. Yes, you read correctly; he was 96! Harry Bernstein began writing his first book, *The Invisible Wall: A Love Story That Broke Barriers*, when he was ninety-three years old. He would then become famous as a writer when he was 96 years old, after his work was published in 2007. The book is about his memories of when he was a child and lived with a poor Jewish family in a mill town in northern England. He wrote three more books in his lifetime. The first one is called *The Dream*, which was published in 2008. The second one is called *The Golden Willow*, published in 2009. The last book, titled *What Happened to Rose*, was published after he died in 2012. There is nothing stopping you! Believe in yourself.

2. **Gladys Burrill**: Marathon runner at 92. I am sure many of you would have been told not to do something like this! But look at Gladys! Gladys Burrill started running marathons when she was 86 years old. She became well-known when she achieved the world record for being the oldest woman to complete a marathon at the age of 92. In 2012, she walked very fast and jogged during the Honolulu Marathon, and it took her nine hours and 53 minutes to finish the race. When she was asked why she was successful, she said it was because she stays active and achieves things by having a positive attitude and a good view of life.

3. **Anna Mary Robertson-Moses**: Painter at 78. Anna Mary Robertson Moses, better known as Grandma Moses by many, started painting in her late 70s. In her early years, she had always imagined being a painter. However, her hectic schedule as a housekeeper, farm laborer, mother, and wife prevented her from pursuing her true passion until much later in life. She had a very fruitful career in the arts and lived to be 101 years old. One of her paintings, Sugaring Off, sold for $1.2 million in 2006, signifying how well-loved her art is even now. The beautiful thing about Anna Mary Roberston-Moses was that she went back to her true passion. This stresses my point that it is never too late to revisit a passion you had but, for whatever reason, could not pursue it at that time.

4. **Peter Mark Roget**: Published lexicographer at 73. You might have used Roget's Thesaurus at some point in your life, but did you know that the author was 73 years old when it was originally released? Roget's Thesaurus of English Words and Phrases was first printed in

1852. Using the initial classifications Roget developed, it would grow to be the most frequently used thesaurus in the English language, and new versions are still being released today. Look at how many of us gained knowledge from using the thesaurus. It might sound cliché, but in the words of Oscar Wilde, with age comes wisdom.

5. **Laura Ingalls Wilder**: Published writer at 65. Laura Ingalls Wilder wrote her series *Little House*, which was based on her childhood, which she spent in a modest Wisconsin home between 1870 and 1894 as a kid of a pioneer family. She released eight volumes in the series as a result of her books' great popularity. The well-known television series Little House on the Prairie, which aired from 1974 to 1983, was based on her novels. I am sure many of you grew up watching *Little House on the Prairie*; it is a true classic! But Laura Ingalls Wilder wrote her stories in her sixties, and look how they took off! If you are reading this and want to pursue writing, do not doubt yourself. You never know what the outcome will be.

6. **Harland Sanders**: Started Kentucky Fried Chicken (KFC) at sixty-two. Harland Sanders, better known worldwide as Colonel Sanders, founded Kentucky Fried Chicken when he was 62 years old. At the age of 74, he decided to sell the company along with his proprietary blend of eleven herbs and spices for $2 million ($18.9 million today). Being one of the biggest fast-food businesses in the world, the corporation still uses his name and likeness as iconic images. KFC is delicious and a super successful franchise! He did not start this business in his thirties or twenties; he was sixty-two.

Please do not dismiss the idea of becoming a business owner in your fifties or older.

7. **Ray Kroc**: He became McDonald's owner at 59. Ray Kroc achieved success in the fast-food sector when he acquired his first McDonald's restaurant from the McDonald brothers at the age of 49. He then led it to become the most prosperous fast-food firm in the world and a franchise on a worldwide scale. Ray Kroc became a multi-millionaire during his lifetime because of his McDonald's franchise. Nothing is stopping you from starting your own franchise if that is what you are interested in.

8. **Julia Child**: She became a celebrity chef at age 51. With her best-selling book, *Mastering the Art of French Cooking*, Julia Child is known for introducing the American audience to French food. The French Chef became a popular television culinary program she later created, which helped her become well-known in America. All of these accomplishments, though, came much later in life. Following her passing in 2004, she became very popular again after a movie starring Meryl Streep and Amy Adams called Julie and Julia was released in 2009. There are many of you who probably dream of sharing your mom's recipes or even your own that you crafted in a book, but put your thoughts on paper and let them flow.

9. **Charles Darwin**. He wrote and published *The Theory of Evolution* at 50. Charles Darwin is one of history's most well-known naturalists and scientists. According to his theory, all living things are descended from a common ancestor. When he was 50 years old, Darwin finally published his idea in his book *On the Origin of*

Species. On the Origin of Species, which he published in 1870. Eleven years after the release of his book, the scientific community has come to embrace his theory of evolution as reality. His idea had a significant influence on modern science as we know it today and was ground-breaking. Let me stress it one more time: Your age does not define you; make your dreams a reality.

10. **Momofuku Ando**: Created the instant noodle at fifty. He is famous for creating instant noodles; Momofuku Ando is an entrepreneur and inventor. He didn't create the instant noodle until he was 50 years old, though! He created the cup noodle at the age of 61. He came up with the brilliant idea to put his instant noodles in a polystyrene water-resistant cup. Water was the only thing you needed to add. He developed Top Ramen and Cup Noodles, two wildly popular products, with his idea. Instant noodles gained popularity all over the world, causing this to become a worldwide industry. He credited playing daily rounds of golf and eating cup noodles for his long life; he lived a long life and died at the age of 96.

I hope that reading these success stories will make you really give thought to planting your creative seed and watching it bloom. Always be patient with yourself. It may be difficult at first, but release your mind from the negative stereotypes that are attached to aging.

PURSUING LIFELONG LEARNING OPPORTUNITIES

You might have the impression that education is something that should only take place when you are young, but it is essential to keep learning as you age. It is advantageous to attempt new things as an older adult, develop new skills, or engage in new hobbies. I have listed the top advantages of lifelong learning for seniors below:

1. **Enhances mental ability and health**: A deterioration in your general cognitive health is a problem that many elderly people encounter. This may make it challenging to comprehend basic ideas and subjects. Continuous learning keeps your mind sharp and stops cognitive decline in its tracks, which is incredible. Seniors' cognitive capacities might continue to be robust when they are regularly taught new concepts or skills. Aging men and women can benefit from lifelong learning by improving their memory and recall abilities. Older people frequently have memory loss and issues remembering things, which makes it challenging for them to recall specific details. Learning new things on a regular basis, like a new language or new technology, can help you maintain your memory and sharpen your recall abilities for longer.

2. **Enhances feelings of happiness and contentment**: As I discussed in Chapters 1 and 2, feeling alone and going through loneliness is something that some seniors experience when living alone. Sadness or despair is difficult for any human to deal with and intensifies with seniors. By focusing on new talents or hobbies, lifelong

learning can improve your overall mood. When you get the opportunity to perform new tasks, you will notice an increase in your self-esteem and confidence. Such tasks could include tending to a garden or performing minor home repairs.

3. **Encourages social interaction**: When you pursue life-long learning, you reap several rewards, among them the strengthening of social engagement. Many senior citizens experience social isolation and find it difficult to interact with others. You may find it easier to interact with others and meet new acquaintances who share your interests by picking up new hobbies or talents. Painting, sewing, or cooking are all enjoyable hobbies that can boost social interaction. A gratifying social network can be formed by taking on a new task or developing a new pastime which introduces you to people in your community.

4. **Increases activity levels**: The value of lifelong learning extends beyond your psychological health. In fact, lifelong learning can help you physiologically as well. There are some seniors who may give up living an inactive lifestyle. Additionally, a significant absence of exercise can have negative effects on your physical and mental health. You can spend your time being active by taking up new hobbies or participating in new activities. You should avoid an inactive lifestyle and increase your physical activity levels to enhance your health by participating in activities like yoga or dancing.

Ways You Can Learn New Skills

Your age does not define you! You can learn whatever you put your mind to; all you need is passion, concentration, and some useful learning techniques. Here is a collection of suggestions and techniques that can assist you in acquiring any new skill you choose, from cooking to learning a foreign language (Flicker, 2023):

1. **Use a variety of sources to educate yourself**: The best learning resources change depending on the skill you wish to master. You may pick up new skills without spending money on a class or instructor! Get whatever you require and look for a few trustworthy sites that can help you learn. This covers textbooks, tutorial videos on the internet, podcasts, etc. Search online for sources, and if you are not tech-savvy, visit your local library for books that will be of use. For instance, there are many resources accessible if you wish to master painting. Visit the library to get books on painting methods, and search YouTube for videos on painting. Every fresh knowledge source is helpful! Don't read just one how-to book; employing a variety of learning techniques to practice a skill might be much more effective than using just one.

2. **Utilize real-world experiences to learn and gain knowledge**: Sometimes, the best way to learn to do something is simply to do it. Although books and tutorials provide fantastic starting points, attempt to use the new skill as soon as you can. Instead of spending all of your time on theory and memorization, learn by making mistakes. Utilize the concepts you have learned

in class or whatever method you learned to determine what functions best for you in practice.

3. **Take a course in person or check out online classes**: Classes provide in-depth, supervised training in what you desire to pursue; it could be learning an instrument, learning a new language, singing, dancing, etc. Look up class options at your neighborhood community college or at nearby churches, free schools, community leisure centers, and cultural institutions. For independent tutors and teachers, look in your neighborhood's periodicals and internet directories.

4. **Teach someone else. Yes, this method is actually helpful**: You can gain a deeper understanding of a skill by teaching it. Why? In order to teach someone else something, you must first critically evaluate the subject or skill in question and divide it into manageable chunks for the person to understand. Practice breaking down each subject into simple stages before teaching others how to do the skill you selected. You can comprehend something better if you can express it well.

5. **Set up a study or practice schedule**: You can stay dedicated to your new endeavor by having a strategy. Establish a practice regimen and adhere to it when learning a new skill. Invest at least 20 hours in mastering the skill; studies suggest that doing so will significantly increase your knowledge and proficiency in any skill. Choose days with lots of spare time and the times of day when you feel most alert to practice.

6. **Remove all distractions**: Procrastination and other forms of distraction can sometimes be blamed for

people's inability to persevere in learning a new skill. Eliminating all temptations reduces your likelihood of becoming sidetracked. Everyone has experienced starting a task and getting sidetracked by something else. It's completely natural and, luckily, preventable. Find a space free from distractions, such as phones and TVs, and avoid using social media or email while doing your new skill. Additionally, avoid multitasking because it lowers your total productivity.

7. **Test yourself**: You may find out how much of the information you recall by taking a test. While taking tests isn't always the most enjoyable thing to do, there are instances when they are necessary. As soon as you master a new concept or skill, give yourself a test. A practice test can be found online, or you can create your own test and grading criteria to use for it. Exams allow you to gauge your level of understanding of the subject and identify any areas that may still need improvement.

8. **Celebrate your accomplishments when they occur**: If you give yourself rewards for accomplishments, you'll be more motivated. Set realistic learning objectives for yourself, and then treat yourself when you reach each one. Instead of waiting for a single, huge reward at the end, make sure your goals are gradual and allow for minor incentives along the way. You are more likely to persist in an endeavor over time when there is a clear purpose for doing so.

9. **Develop a skill that you are enthusiastic about**: When you genuinely appreciate the subject, you're more inclined to continue learning. Why not pursue a long-held hobby or learn something that interests you?

Consider the abilities that have always intrigued you or made you wish you had them. It does not have to be about professional development in regards to learning a new skill, but simply to benefit your mental health. Learning can be done just for enjoyment.

DEVELOPING NEW HOBBIES

Learning new hobbies is not only fun, but they are also a great way to keep you busy and are also great at allowing your mind to shift focus. It is a great way to combat feelings of loneliness and prevent self-isolation, along with keeping your wonderful mind active. Taking up hobbies will bring you such high levels of elation, and it will enhance your life. We are living in a time when we have so many things that are accessible to us. Using your laptop or your phone, you search for a particular hobby or interest. In fact, there are websites and various pages on Instagram and Facebook that are devoted strictly to hobbies and interests; there are endless possibilities.

You are all unique and have various things that you are interested in. Even as I list things that you could think about exploring, at the end of the day, you may end up not finding anything listed to your liking. The key thing that I want to emphasize is that I want you all to look into yourself and truly figure out what you are truly interested in and what works best for you. It could be something that you were once very passionate about as a child or young adult and never got a chance to explore, or it could be something that is new but exciting to you and makes your heart and spirit excited. What is even more amazing is that once you find what you are truly enamored with, it will engulf you, and you will love every second of it. It will become a part of you.

Take a look at these advantageous reasons you should have at least one hobby:

1. It makes it easier to be more social and interesting. Now, I am not telling you that people's opinions matter. But there are some of you who get a bit nervous around meeting new people and tend not to know what to say. When you have a new hobby, let's say you start playing the guitar; it is a great icebreaker. Sharing with people the knowledge you have gained so far is a great topic of conversation, and you may even meet someone who is also learning how to use a musical instrument.

2. It is a great stress reliever. Life is stressful enough, and even though you are now a senior or maybe a retiree, that does not mean that stress disappears. At each stage in our lives, we encounter new issues. Taking on a new hobby allows your mind to chill out. You will receive solace in your new activity, and it gives you something else to think about outside of paying taxes and bills.

3. Hobbies will help with your patience level. Hobbies do, in fact, allow you to gain patience. The reason is that because you are learning something new that is out of your comfort zone, it will enable you to learn to be more patient with yourself. This level of patience will melt into your everyday life; you will find that you will

not be so irritated waiting in the doctor's office for too long or waiting to pick up your prescription.

4. Hobbies open up your social circle. Remember at the beginning that hobbies are great for icebreakers and speaking with someone with the same interest? Well, it does not have to end there; it could be that you joined a club or that one conversation about playing the guitar opens the door to a new friendship.

5. Hobbies are great confidence boosters. Nothing beats getting something new! It makes you feel good, and it makes you feel better about yourself. It is always great to celebrate those wins! You are a winner!

6. Hobbies help to minimize or remove boredom. Being bored stinks! As you get older, you are not out and about as you used to. Not that you are boring, but there are certain things that you may not do anymore, and there are days you may find yourself at home wondering what to do, or it may be that your life is getting a bit too routine. What a hobby does: It removes that; it is a great way to occupy your time, and it also gives you something to look forward to.

7. You blossom and learn new skills. You will only get better at this new skill you are learning, and that will always be a win. Once you decide to invest your time, you will notice that you will be led in a direction that will build new and useful skills.

8. You will have an increase in knowledge. This is always a great aspect! Aside from the new skills, your knowledge level will grow. Continuous learning is always a plus in anything, regardless of age.

9. It changes your outlook on life. Regardless of the hobby you choose, the plus is that it unveils fresh ideas. You will evolve in a variety of ways, and this includes changing your perspective on life.

10. It will take you out of your comfort zone and challenge you. In life, you should never get too comfortable; it will leave you in a stage of life where you do not develop. It is always great to challenge yourself, so pick a hobby that is new and challenging. If your hobby is not that challenging, you will find that you won't stay with it for long, or you will notice that you will start finding it boring. Our minds are meant to be challenged. You can handle it. The more engaging and challenging, the more you will want to remain and learn.

11. It keeps you engaged so that you won't waste time. If you are not careful, you will find yourself wasting time on social media and not using that energy and your brainpower for other things. Hobbies are an excellent way to fill that time, and you will gain so much more from them than from watching 3,000 memes.

HOBBIES THAT MAY SPARK YOUR INTEREST

1. **Reading**: I list reading because many of you did not like reading or did not do that much reading growing up. You can read anything you want; it could be romance novels or books on building a business after fifty. Find something that is engaging.

2. **Cooking**: There is nothing like learning new recipes or creating your own spin on a dish. If you are someone who has never really cooked, this hobby could be per-

fect for you. It also adds to the independence factor. If you are someone who loves to cook but has never baked a cake or cookie before, this is where you can challenge yourself. Do not worry if the first attempt at the cake is burned; you will get better at it, I promise.

3. **Watching documentaries**: I picked documentaries as a hobby because there are so many, and you can learn new things. Whether it is something about nature on National Geographic or a murder mystery. You gain something from it. I should also include that watching a DIY series is also helpful and can give you ideas for your home.

4. **Exercising**: I am all for keeping active. Try aqua aerobics, Zumba dancing, or Latin dancing. The list for this is endless. It is not limited to jogs and walks, especially if it is an activity you have never done before.

5. **Gardening**: Gardening can give you not only tranquility but also nothing like seeing the fruits of your labor. Growing tomatoes and seeing them grow, as well as planting edible things, cuts costs when going to the supermarket. If you love flowers, seeing them bloom and the range of colors will make your eyes and spirit do backflips.

Hobbies are very fulfilling, and they will give you a new sense of purpose and peace and will increase your mood in a positive way. If you have not taken up a new hobby, hop up now and try!

KEY TAKEAWAY POINTS

It is clear that older adults need to keep learning throughout their lives, but you may be thinking about how to actually do it. Here are some easy ways to try out new skills or hobbies that you might like (Pardue-Spears, 2022):

- Taking a painting class

- Trying new food recipes

- Starting a garden

- Going to a dance class or practicing dance moves at home

- Making minor repairs to your home

- Getting more acquainted with technology

- Taking a yoga class

- Practicing meditation

- Personal involvement is the finest approach to incorporating education and learning into your daily lives. You will experience the advantages of lifelong learning in your life if you attempt new talents and pastimes with a family member, friend, or caregiver. The benefits are definitely worth the work.

A LONG HEALTHY AND HAPPY LIFE

What is the secret to a long, healthy, and happy life? Is there a secret to a long and healthy life? Do you want to live for a very long time? Pardon me for flooding you with these thought-provoking questions, but I am sure many of you have had these questions float around in your mind at some point. Some people have embraced the idea that their time will end one day, and they are quite content with it. At the same time, there are some of you for whom the thought of reaching a certain age and your existence freaks you out. Also, aside from that, aging and not looking how you once did, do not sit well with some of you, while others embrace their wrinkles and love their gray hair. I am saying all this to say that all of what you are feeling is normal; it does not make you weird. We are all human beings, and we think differently. We all have a different outlook on life when it comes to various things, not just aging and solo living. But there is somewhat of a secret to living longer and healthier. With all the advancements in science, it seems that scientists may soon discover the fountain of youth. Exciting right? But the major question you may have is how it is possible for us to live longer and healthier when we are getting older. I mean, we are human beings, not vampires. There is absolutely nothing at this moment that can pause the age you are and not make you get older.

Cellular senescence is the physiological process that results in a gradual decline in cell functioning and causes our organisms to age. Due to the fact that human beings will always be on the quest for longevity, it is no surprise that research centers and many biomedical companies are exploring ways to significantly slow down or perhaps halt the aging process altogether. Science has evolved significantly with time, and today, science involves working with nanoparticles, mending DNA, rebuilding cells, and creating tissues and organs from stem cells. There are some researchers whose life's goal is to improve the cognitive capabilities of human beings by fusing computer components with our cells and neurons (*The science of longevity*, 2017).

Think about it for a second. This is something we have seen in movies or read in fictional books, and it seems like it could almost become a reality. Take, for example, the reinjection of autologous stem cells for cosmetic or regenerative medicine. Examining living things proved to be exceedingly difficult for a very long time. Cells, tissues, and organs require a great deal of care when being examined and worked on. We were just not there yet. The task of comprehending our biological processes appeared overwhelming. However, due to how technology has evolved, it has managed to transform medical research. Genome sequencing used to cost $3 billion, but it is now more affordably priced, enabling more personalized treatment. But alas, we are not all created equally, and what may work well for one person may not work at all for another. So, one of the cornerstones of this science of longevity is personalized genetic mapping. Our biological age, which results from causes and makes preventative medicine possible, is what is defined rather than our chronological age (*The science of longevity*, 2017).

THE LIFESTYLE OF A SUPER-AGER

Now, super-agers did not find a magic serum that allowed them to get to this stage; they have certain lifestyle practices that they exhibit. If you are interested in being a member of this elite club, have a look at the list of habits exhibited by super-agers. Maybe you can make some adjustments to your life, or maybe you are already on your way to becoming a super-ager. The thing I want you all to keep in mind is that not only are these people in their eighties and older, but they are coherent and functioning members of society.

No one wants to make it to their eighties when they are not in a great physiological and psychological state:

1. **Super-agers have active lifestyles**: Now you see how everything I have mentioned before about starting a new hobby, getting a new skill, and keeping active all tie into place. I cannot stress this enough, but keeping active is, in fact, one of the greatest things you can do for yourself as you get older. Your body will receive more oxygen when you are exercising; what this does is assist in healthy body performance. There are other amazing positives; your heart will benefit, and we all want our hearts to be happy. It is observed that older people who are more active tend to have fewer instances where they fall, including during muscle-strengthening activities. Also, ensuring that you exercise on a regular basis helps to maintain a healthy weight. Being overweight or obese comes with a barrage of health issues, such as diabetes and hypertension, to name

a few. Also, making exercise a part of your life lowers your risk of developing Alzheimer's disease. In fact, Alzheimer's disease not only doubles but triples in people who have a body mass index (BMI) that is over thirty. If I could place the shock emoji here, I would. If you decide to work out twice a week, it will be a great help to you and decrease your chance of developing the disease later in life.

2. **Super-agers tend to challenge themselves**: Your mind needs to always be learning, and being challenged mentally is just as important as being physically active. Your mind is endless, and your age does not define you. Get into the habit of stepping out of your comfort zone and learning new things. If you are not big on mind games, try learning a new hobby or skill. Take on reading a book that is not something you would normally read to feed your brain; it will pay off in the long term.

3. **Super-agers tend to be social beings**: This is why I made sure to speak about isolation and what to avoid. Being around others is great for you! Super-agers tend to be folks who have strong ties with people around them. Maintaining a strong social network tends to be very beneficial for you. From a scientific standpoint, there is a region in our brains called the attention region, and it was found that with super-agers, this region was greater. To delve even deeper, this area has many long and thin neurons called von Economo neurons. These neurons are believed to help us understand and interact with others in social situations. Autopsies on super-agers showed that they have many more of these special brain cells compared to most people in their eighties (Roglaski, 2023).

The Path to Longevity

Until an age-stopping serum is invented, or the fountain of youth is discovered, you have to start practicing healthy ways that will be beneficial to you and be great contributing factors to your longevity. Your nutrition is important, as is exercising your mind and body, as this can increase your life expectancy. But there is more to it than just that; you have to avoid overeating and be mindful of your alcohol consumption. Doing so lowers your risk of certain illnesses and keeps your body healthy, and with a healthy body and mind, you will live longer.

Listed below are other habits you can choose to incorporate into your life that will help you along your path to longevity:

1. **Overeating is a no-no**: Overeating over time results in weight gain, which is bad for your heart, among other things. The more weight you gain, the less active you become. According to research conducted on animals, reducing normal calorie intake by 10–50% may lengthen maximum longevity (Fontana, 2010). When you make the decision to reduce your calorie intake, you get to a healthier weight, and if you have some belly fat, that will go down as well. These things are all positive and will be beneficial to you on your path to longevity.

2. **Nuts are the best**: Making nuts a part of your daily diet is great for your body and your heart. Nuts are amazing because they contain unsaturated fatty acids and other essential nutrients. Some of you who are reading this are probably snackers. I mean, who does not love a

good snack? However, many people who tend to snack tend to love consuming unhealthy snacks. Putting nuts on your snack list will satisfy that snack craving, and they are also healthy and inexpensive. It is a win–win situation. However, I should note that there are some nuts that are high in calories, so ensure you have control over your portions. Let me just list some other benefits of consuming nuts:

- It boosts your artery health—a happy heart leads to a happy and longer life.

- It decreases your chances of heart disease-related inflammation. I am sure your heart leaped as you read that part.

- It lowers the chance of blood clots forming, which can cause heart attacks and strokes.

- It lessens the chance of getting high blood pressure.

3. **Learn a new trick and try some turmeric**: I cannot be on the topic of longevity and not bring your attention to turmeric. Turmeric is an amazing option. This spice contains an effective bioactive element called curcumin. What is curcumin, you ask? Curcumin is, in fact, the main component of turmeric, and it can lessen inflammation. According to a number of studies, it may reduce painful and inflammatory osteoarthritis and rheumatoid arthritis symptoms (Griffin, 2021).

4. **Don't forget your greens and fruits**: Sometimes, many people neglect to include plant-based foods in their diet, and in doing so, they rob their bodies of need-

ed nutrients and other much-needed vitamins. Do not forget to include fruits, vegetables, nuts, beans, and whole grains when you prepare your foods; they supply your body with so much and are an excellent factor when it comes to longevity.

5. **Get on a bicycle and enjoy the outdoors**: Okay, so you do not have to get on a bicycle, but, at this point, it should not be surprising that you are getting physical made it on the list. Staying physically active adds years to your life. You will look and feel good inwardly and outwardly.

6. **Put that cigarette down**: Smoking is a no-no! It is not good for your heart or lungs, among other things. There are people who smoke and end up developing respiratory problems, and smoking is linked to lung cancer. Smoking cuts your life short, and this does not fit in on the longevity path.

7. **A little wine never hurt anybody**: I am not telling anyone that having a glass of wine is a no-no. Here is the thing with alcohol: It should be consumed moderately. No one should be drinking to get wasted, drinking every day, or drinking four to six glasses of any alcoholic beverage. Think about your liver; high levels of alcohol consumption have been linked to liver, heart, and pancreatic diseases.

8. **Stress is not the best**: High levels of stress and anxiety can affect your body negatively. Stress can give you migraines and affect your mood, leading to depression, etc. Stress should always be kicked out of your house. However, on a realistic scale, stress will occur no matter what. The key is how you handle it. Mindfulness,

meditation, and yoga are great ways of letting stress exit the building and giving your mind clarity to deal with the situation that has arisen. The key thing is not basking in the situation and letting it take over; that is giving stress way more power and control than it deserves when you are the one in control. Also, stress ages you more, and we are not about that.

9. **Sleep is your best friend**: Resting your body is the best thing ever. Getting to bed at a good time and getting the adequate hours of sleep that you need will have you waking up feeling exuberant and fresh! Not getting enough sleep tends to affect your mood; you will notice that you are more irritated and having a difficult time focusing on things. That's because your body needs that rest! Try to get 7-8 hours of sleep. Also, if you oversleep, that could be linked to depression or other health issues. Please reach out to someone if this is happening, and more importantly, contact your healthcare provider. Another thing is to practice not using your phone in bed during the time you plan on sleeping, as this can be a distraction and keep you up later than you initially planned. If you plan on sleeping at 9:30 p.m., start making your way into your room at 9:00 p.m. That way, you will be in La La Land by 9:30 p.m. If you wait until 9:30 p.m. to start making your way to your room, you will end up falling asleep later than planned.

KEY TAKEAWAY POINTS

- A happy and healthy life is not a fairytale and can actually become a reality for you.

- Longevity is not difficult, but it will require you to make some changes to your life. There are many healthy habits that can lead you on the path to longevity and make you a super-ager.

- Being a super-ager is achievable!

- Get enough sleep; rest is always best.

- Practice various techniques that will kick stress to the curb.

- Consume alcohol in moderation. Your liver and heart will love you unconditionally for it.

- When combined, these behaviors can improve your health and set you up for a long, happy, and healthy life.

WISDOM AND REFLECTION

Your past is in the past; however, your past helped shape the person you are now, but do not let your past mistakes make you feel as if you are worthless or a bad person. You cannot rewind; you can only move forward. With every experience you had, you learned something from it. Whether you learned it immediately or later in your life. The key thing is that you learned. Your seed of wisdom was planted, and now the tree has grown significantly, and on your tree lie the fruits of knowledge and wisdom.

DO NOT LIVE IN THE PAST; LEARN FROM IT

What we have experienced in the past has shaped who we are now. Life is unpredictable; we have all experienced both positive and negative events. These events are contributing factors to how we view the world, people, and ourselves. It can be what makes some of us leaders adaptable and receptive to change, and in some cases, it makes some of us suffer from anxiety issues, not being well at problem-solving, being passive-aggressive, etc. But let me look at how the past shapes who you are today.

Your past shapes the senior you are today in impactful ways. Some of the areas of your past that can affect your life are:

1. **Your past is a contributing factor to your personality**: If you are not careful, you can be stuck in the past and not grow from it, and instead of learning, you repeat the same thing even as an older person. So, your past can impact you either negatively or positively. I

want to lean towards the positive for all of you. Your personality traits and various habits are formed from your past. For example, if you had a family member who died in a plane crash when you were younger, you may end up having a fear of flying and will never step foot on a plane. Also, your past experiences can have an influence on various things that you take an interest in. You may have had a parent who loved taking you to museums and art shows, and you end up falling in love with the Victorian period.

2. **Your past plays a major role in how you handle relationships**: Your past can influence your current relationships. Things that happened to you in your past can have a major impact on your romantic life, how you and your family interact, and your friendships. These various things can impact how you handle conflict, rejection, etc. It can also affect new love interests because you may have been through a messy divorce, and your spouse was unfaithful, so you will struggle with trust issues.

3. **Your past can impact your overall health and well-being**: Having unresolved issues can affect you on a psychological level; it can be the reason you have high levels of anxiety and paranoia and are not good at dealing with stress. You already know how I feel about stress; it is a big no-no. However, it does happen, and I want you all to be able to manage it in a healthy way as opposed to letting it take over your entire life. Stress, depression, and anxiety can cause other illnesses that can impact your health negatively.

4. **Your past can influence your career choice and your sense of purpose in life**: Something that you witnessed

or experienced in the past may lead you to choose a particular career or field of study. For instance, if you witnessed a friend or family member drowning and you initially wanted to be a lawyer, but due to that incident, you may end up shifting your goals and decide that you now want to be a swimming instructor or a paramedic. Also, past experience can contribute to your sense of purpose. Due to witnessing those traumatic examples listed above, you may end up having a strong desire to help people through similar experiences and end up in the field of psychology. Your past experiences help you discover who you truly are if you are open and willing to learn from those experiences. These experiences, whether they are negative or positive, can help you learn what your character strengths and weaknesses are and what you need to work on.

5. **Your past influences have ethnic and societal impacts**: What happened in your past can affect both your cultural and societal lives in a variety of ways. Your values, beliefs, and feelings about certain things stem from past experiences. Sometimes, you are not even aware of them; they can happen on a subconscious level or on a more profound level. If you are part of a specific culture or community, you may find that you have a strong bond with that group and tend not to want to interact with many people outside of that group. The same thing applies to your views toward social justice problems, including racial justice, environmental action, and gender equality. These opinions can be influenced by your prior experiences. You may also be prompted by prior events to question or rebel against certain societal or cultural standards. When some

habits or beliefs go against your gut instinct or inner direction, you may experience discomfort or resistance. As a result, you could decide to demand change or oppose the existing condition.

When you take the time to reflect on these various experiences, you will be able to ascertain certain patterns and lessons that can allow you to truly discover who you are and allow your wisdom tree to bring forth more fruits of knowledge and wisdom.

DEALING WITH THE PAST

Seeing that there has not been a time machine invented yet, we cannot go back in time and change certain things. I mean, would you really want to change certain things and miss the lessons you learned from them? However, the reality is that the past is in the past; this is not a movie, and we cannot press the rewind, pause, or stop button. If you allow yourself to relive the past and replay scenarios that you cannot change, you will only upset yourself or make yourself sad and stuck on a beach, swimming in the sea of regret and hopelessness. That is not a fun beach to visit, in my opinion. Reframing and managing our perceptions of unfavorable situations is possible in a variety of ways.

Do not live your life in robot mode. There are many situations that we encounter daily, and without being aware of them, we react instinctively because our minds have gotten used to simply going through the motions. You have now become that person who lives their life without being aware or truly living. Avoid becoming almost like a robot; be in the present; do not just go through the motions.

Do not allow negative things that happened in your life to become your narrative. Avoid making negative situations define you and being a part of your everyday life and then allowing them to mold the person you are now in a negative way. See these bad moments or experiences as things that occurred; in other words, view them as something that happened on a particular day, in a specific month and year, during a certain period in your life, and it is not who you are.

Focus on your good experiences and accomplishments. Always remember those good and happy moments, remember the feelings they gave you, and use that energy in your present situation. Always use those good moments as encouragement.

Use your past experiences to help others. Remember what I said about your wisdom seed? Now, this is how it can be of great use. You can use your life experiences as a way to counsel or guide others. If you have been in a similar situation, you can guide that person so they do not make the same mistake you did, or if they make a similar mistake, you will be able to walk them through it, especially if they feel hopeless and as if they cannot make it. Your words of encouragement and guidance will go a long way. It will also do something for you internally, knowing that you helped someone through a tough situation with your guidance and leadership.

Let it go... Let it go. Do not harbor animosity towards others. Holding onto grudges and ill feelings towards people will have you stuck in a vortex of negativity. Who wants that? These feelings can end up making you feel bitter and resentful, and before you know it, you have now become the mean old person across the street. In some cases, holding on to those feelings will end up making you into the very person who did you wrong. Forgiveness is not for the other person; it is for you and your peace of mind.

Look at your past as a learning experience. Imagine you are watching a movie, and they go back to a scene from something that happened ten years ago, and the main character is thinking back on what he or she should or could have done differently to pass a test or save their dog from getting hit by a car. As they are reliving it, they realize what they could have done differently, and because of that, they are even more cautious with the pet they own now, or they have taught their children better study methods. I want you to do the same thing. Your past is a learning experience; learn from it and make better decisions in your present state. In doing so, it will help you live a fuller, more peaceful, and more content life.

With acceptance comes balance. Acceptance is such a powerful and beautiful word. When you learn to accept what has occurred and understand that there is nothing you can do but move on, you will find how much better you will feel.

Be in the present and control your thoughts. Mindfulness and meditation would be great tools for this because when you allow your mind to drift into the past, that is when you can let those thoughts control you, and you will find that you feel helpless. You are in control; regain that control and authority, and you will find how much better you feel mentally.

The Power of Self-Reflection

As we all get older, all our physical, spiritual, emotional, and psychological needs shift. This is normal; what you enjoyed in your thirties may not be what you will enjoy in your fifties, and what you enjoyed in your fifties may not be what you are drawn to in your sixties. It is called growth and as a human being, with feelings, emotions, etc. Our moods and desires change. Self-reflection is an important component that is oftentimes overlooked by seniors. Self-reflection is the practice of looking deep into yourself and observing or examining your deep thoughts, feelings, and life experiences. I know, I know, I just spoke about letting go of the past and not letting it hold you back, but self-reflection is not on the wavelength. The thing to keep in mind about self-reflection is that it is a key facet of personal maturity and exceedingly advantageous, especially for seniors.

I will be delving deeper into why self-reflection should be an intricate part of your life as a senior and how it can ameliorate your overall well-being:

1. **You will have a better understanding of yourself**: Self-reflection is such a useful and strong tool that can help you have a better understanding of yourself. In

this phase of your life, being older and taking time to think about your thoughts, feelings, and various experiences, you can see patterns, learn from them, and be cognizant of why you act in a particular way. Tapping into this can bring to light a true understanding of yourself and can help you make better decisions and have better relationships with others.

2. **Self-reflection can help with the reduction of stress and anxiety**: Stress is never a great thing, regardless of where we are in our lives. However, it seems that as we get older, feeling stressed and anxious can happen more often. Have you noticed that? When this happens, it can make you feel less happy and healthy overall. Self-reflection can assist you in understanding why you are feeling so stressed and anxious. In doing this, it can help you learn how to deal with these emotions and find ways to decrease stressors in your daily life. By understanding what makes you feel upset, agitated, nervous, or overwhelmed, you can make your home a more calm and peaceful place to live in.

3. **It can help with increasing your gratitude and positivity levels**: The beauty of self-reflection is that it makes you focus on the positive. Thinking about yourself and focusing on the good things that have occurred in your life will make you feel more grateful, which will, in turn, feed your positivity levels. Positivity does wonders for your mood, soul, and body. Thinking about and appreciating the good things in your life will make you feel better and happier, and nothing feels better than that.

4. **Your relationships with others will improve**: No one is perfect; we all have flaws and things that we need to

work on. We all have certain ways that we have inter-acted with people that we are not proud of. The reason self-reflection is such a great tool is that it allows you to think about your relationships with others. You can then learn how to make those relationships better. Self-reflection can help you recognize problems with talking to and understanding others and focus on why it is that you and certain people argue, or why you can be so snappy with certain folks, or even tap into why you are a passive-aggressive person, or even why you tend to avoid addressing certain matters when it comes to some people. What self-reflection can do in regards to all of this is help you figure out how to solve these problems. You are getting older; I know none of you want to be known as the Grinch. Getting along better with people will contribute to your having a happier and more meaningful life.

5. **It can increase your cognitive performance level**: I want all of you to enjoy these years and have not only your body functioning well but your beautiful minds as well. Thinking about yourself and your sea of thoughts can, in fact, improve your cognitive performance. When you take those few moments to think about yourself, it can sharpen your memory, focus, and ability to solve problems. If your brain is still functioning well and you are coherent, it will allow you to remain independent and have a better life.

TIPS FOR SELF-REFLECTION

If you are truly interested in self-reflection, there are many things you can do to get started. Here are a few tips to help you get started:

- **It is best not to just randomly start**: You should set aside some time each day for your self-reflection session and take this time to think about yourself and your actions. You can start with a few minutes each day and gradually increase the time. If you want to keep it for a few minutes, nothing is wrong with that either; this is your journey, and the only narrator is you. Take your self-reflection time to think about your thoughts, emotions, and things that have happened in your life.

- **Journaling**: Write your thoughts, experiences, and feelings as they come to you, and allow everything to flow out of you onto paper. When you write down what you think and feel, it can help you understand things better and notice similarities. Journaling is a great way to look back and compare and contrast your notes.

- **Seek counseling**: I have to highlight that there are certain things that have occurred to some of you that are so traumatic that you will need guidance as you go through this process of self-reflection. Here is where I will advise you to speak to someone who can help you with your problems or emotional well-being, like a therapist or counselor. A therapist or counselor can help you by giving advice and being there for you as you think about and understand yourself better.

- **Practice mindfulness and meditation**: I am a huge advocate for practicing mindfulness and meditation. By engaging in meditation and mindfulness techniques will enable you to improve your level of concentration and feed your body relaxation, along with simplifying the process of introspection and understanding your own emotions.

RESILIENCE

Now, we are going to dive into the river of resilience. All of you are resilient and have displayed it in many ways. Being resilient involves combining your grief with self-awareness and compassion for yourself and others. Our collective human experience during the COVID-19 pandemic has shown how crucial it is to keep our hearts and minds open so that we can communicate with one another in innovative ways and share our experiences of bravery and resiliency. The topic of resilience and how to become more resilient in the midst of difficulty, stress, and exhaustion is one that is frequently brought up in conversations on a regular basis. Things really have changed, and so have we. Resilience is already embedded in us; our ability to bounce back and overcome challenges is a natural part of us as human beings. We have always used our strengths to help us feel grounded and secure, but it takes discipline and patience to develop this skill.

Becoming a resilient person is not something that happens quickly; it comes through experiences and various life lessons. It is totally achievable by consistently working on yourself and reflecting on your personal experiences. The ability to bounce back from difficult situations is tied to your inner courage. We all have that inner courage; some of you are not even aware of it or have even tapped into its full potential. This courage allows you to be open to feeling vulnerable and unsure about what will happen next. However, you have hope and confidence that your resilience will help you keep pushing forward. If you have experienced or are going through tough times at this moment, I want you to know that being strong and resilient requires bravery and self-reflection. In fact, this is why I made it a point of duty to speak about self-reflection before talking about resilience. These two flow together; if there was ever a perfect couple, it would be them.

Being a resilient person shows your strength and is something that takes time to build, even though it can be tiring both psychologically and physiologically. I want to highlight that it takes time to become a resilient person. I hope now you can get how everything ties in together, with me speaking on how your wisdom seed has been planted and has grown and how your past experiences are life experiences to gain knowledge from. All of you reading this are resilient people; you had to develop and mold that part of you over time. I do not think some of you give yourself enough credit; you have been through a lot, and you are still here, being amazing. When you are consistent, your ability to bounce back and overcome challenges becomes a natural part of your character and influences how you respond. The truth is that being resilient requires a person to have a lot of inner strength and learn from difficult experiences. And it's not always a nice experience. Sometimes, difficult and traumatic experiences can help a person become resilient. But does it always have to be difficult? The truth is, it doesn't always have to be if we think about how it can help us in the grand scheme of things. Good leaders have the capability to reflect on their failures and rough times. This is something that all of us do, and what it does is teach us to find strength and wisdom within ourselves. It helps us to connect with our deeper feelings and to boldly take the next step forward.

Being able to transform a very difficult or traumatic experience into a moment of victory is a common and powerful theme in the stories of heroes. Think about it for a second. Take the Batman character, for example. His parents were killed by a villain as a child, and in return, he used that trauma and pain to become a vigilante to help others in distress. He did not end up becoming a villain himself, which he could have done, or he could have carried pain and had feelings of guilt and sadness take over his life (living in the past). You find that you can relate to others who have gone through tough times and see how your own strength and determination have helped you grow. This has helped you embrace creativity and use your energy to lead yourself and inspire others to reach their full potential. There are so many of you walking around who have inspired people in your family, community, and friendship circles. It is something that some of you do not even realize, and a lot of you do not give yourself enough credit. Having a positive mindset is very valuable.

When you are aware and clear about things, having a positive attitude can help you turn a negative situation into a positive one. You should try to think about the good things that could happen, even when you're feeling really down. I know it is difficult, especially as you get older, but it is in you. Also, think about what your inner wisdom tells you. Do not ever forget that you have a tree of wisdom and knowledge that has grown tremendously. Look into yourself. I am not saying that you should avoid feeling sad or brush off a horrible situation like it is nothing; you are a human, not a machine. What I am leaning toward is that the way you talk to yourself and others shows what you believe about your life story. You all have the amazing ability and inner strength to serve a bigger purpose in your lives, even when you are facing difficult challenges. This is a valuable trait to have when you join a community or become a volunteer. When you view your positive attitude as a way to develop your character, you can genuinely support and inspire others to recognize and embrace their own extraordinary abilities.

You should have a list of things you are thankful for, which you look at when you feel like everything is going wrong and you can't find anything good or feel like your positive light is dimming. Having a positive mindset and being thankful for what you have while also being willing to face challenges and think about what you can do to overcome them is an amazing thing to practice. Even if you only have five minutes to yourself to feel better, be thankful for who you are and the talents you can give to others. Be kind to yourself. You went through tough times and faced challenges for a reason. Don't give up on yourself and the people around you. Having a valiant reason for doing something is what will inspire you to stay focused on your goals. Remember, your age does not limit you in achieving greatness. Find the energy to get back up when you feel you have hit rock bottom, and be your guiding light during difficult times. It is the never-ending reason why we do things and the strong motivation that keeps us going. I want to end this segment by talking about how self-leadership is important for all of you.

Self-leadership means allowing yourself the power to succeed. Success comes in various forms; do not compare yourself to others in any way. It involves taking responsibility for your own actions and success and having the perseverance to keep going, even when you feel like giving up. Making it to the age you are is a success in itself; living alone while still functioning and taking care of your responsibilities is a huge success! You can get a lot of help and advice, but in the end, it's up to you to take action and develop the qualities and habits that will make you successful. Alternatively, you might not have the necessary help, and everything may appear challenging, but this is also an important aspect of the learning process. You have learned from challenges in the past, and you will continue to learn from them the older you get. You should be around people who motivate you to be the best you can be. This is why it is important to get involved in your community and avoid social isolation. You can make small choices, like helping someone without expecting anything in return or reading a book about something new and telling someone about it.

When people are arguing with you, you can choose to be peaceful and handle situations calmly. It's important to be kind and do your part to help your community. When you try your best to use your amazing abilities, others see you as a leader and can feel motivated by your decisions. You all have the ability to do this. The great thing is that you can do it in your own special way by being creative and strong. The knowledge and strength you gain from facing your own difficulties will always be valuable to your community because, as humans, we have more in common when it comes to facing challenges and tough times than we think. Don't forget to be nice to yourself and take care of your mental and physical health. Always be kind and patient with yourself. Be open to change and learning new things. Don't be afraid of failure. Instead, see it as a chance to learn and improve. Be brave and believe in yourself. You have the ability to make your dreams come true; your age does not define you.

KEY TAKEAWAY POINTS

- Do not marinate in past experiences; learn from them and grow.

- We all have a story to tell; we are all authors, and our books have many chapters filled with titles and subtitles. As you start this new chapter, it will be new and refreshing, and it will be nothing like the negative tales of your past.

- Self-reflection will help you feel better.

- You will learn more about yourselves through practicing self-reflection.

- You will feel less stressed and anxious through self-reflection.

- You will tap into developing higher levels of gratitude and optimism.

- You will foster healthier connections with others and enhance your cognitive functioning.

- As you embark on this journey of solo living, or if you are already living alone, try to include self-reflection in your daily routine. It will help you experience certain advantages and enhance your overall life quality.

- Remember, you can always prioritize self-reflection and focus on your well-being, as even small actions can significantly impact your overall emotional state.

CONCLUSION

This is a new chapter in your life; you are the author. You are in control of your narrative; take out your pen and begin to write. Living alone is not scary; it is a new journey that you are embarking on, and I believe that you are ready for it! Aging does present challenges; in fact, life overall presents challenges, but it is how we handle them. I want to leave you with some gems to remember any time you feel overwhelmed. I want you to keep these reminders.

THINGS TO KEEP IN MIND WHEN LIVING ALONE

1. **You will not lose your independence**: No one wants to feel like they cannot take care of themselves. It can dampen your whole mood when you lose your independence. Think about how many of you have been living independently for the bulk of your lives, having your careers, raising your family, and just making the everyday decisions that come with adulting. However, there are factors that have changed, whether it is your mobility or health. This can almost make you feel as if a part of you is missing. When you decide to take on solo living regardless of certain constraints, a part of your

independence is still there; you can still make certain decisions, and that within itself feels good.

2. **Your self-esteem will rise, and you will not lose your individualism**: To delve deeper into point one, when you start to feel like you are no longer in control of managing certain tasks and making certain decisions, a part of you starts to feel empty, which almost makes you feel like you are less of a person, and this can lead to depression, self-isolation, anxiety, and other negative things. Living on your own in your personal space gives you back a bit of you, believe it or not. Sometimes, what happens is that you get into your head and start focusing on the alone aspect, and that is not a bad thing. You will still be able to stay in touch with family and friends. Being in your home, you still have control over deciding what color you want your walls painted and where to place photos. You are still in control of what to watch on television, when to go to the park, when to get ice cream, what to wear, and what to eat. That means you are still in control of yourself, and that will make you feel more confident and content within yourself.

3. **Find ways to maintain your balance and strength**: I am not trying to scare anyone, but there have been many cases where seniors lose balance in their homes and fall. This is something I do not want any of you to experience. If you are reading this and have experienced falling. It is important to maintain your balance and strength if you want to continue living alone. This is also a great way to stay active; being inactive is a no-no. Being active helps with your overall health and psychological well-being. You have to get into the hab-

it of strength training. If you are not regularly working on your strength, when you are aging, you will end up losing muscle mass and your core balance. This is where falls occur due to the fact that you have lost your strength and balance, which can lead to frequent falls, which can then lead to long-term injuries that will then lead to you not having the independence that makes you "you."

4. **You will gain a sense of purpose**: Sometimes, you can fall into feeling isolated, which can lead to feelings of hopelessness and depression. Your psychological well-being is very important, and when your mental health is not 100%, it can affect the quality of your life. What I want you all to remember is that living alone is not a bad thing in any way. Do not let your mind play tricks on you. The key word is independence; you will have your sense of purpose and not lose it. You will always be the phoenix that rises from the ashes. That in itself is magnificent. Your life is NOT over; you will realize that new opportunities will present themselves to you; you are still important to your family; and because of your wisdom and experience, you will be the one from whom your younger family members will seek your advice; and you will be able to make new friends and become more acquainted with your neighbors. You will be able to set new goals and achieve them. You will face new challenges that you will solve because you are more than capable of doing so. If you are a senior who has a disability or limited mobility, you are not left out of this; you can still get involved in activities in your community. Your age does not define you (I cannot stress this point enough).

5. **Your memory will improve**: Solo living is also a great contributing factor in enhancing memory skills. Due to the fact that you are living alone and that you are more active and engaging with people around you, you will find that performing your daily routines will foster your memory skills. Also, set up post-it reminders at certain places in your home, and each week, remove them until you do not need them anymore. This will aid your memory.

6. **You will notice that you have a certain level of control**: There are certain things in life we cannot control. Getting older is one of the many things we have no control over. Living on your own helps give you a sense of control because you will be in control of certain things in your home. Such as which day you use to head to the supermarket, what day you want to have visitors over to your home, what book you want to read, and what series you want to watch. You do not have to deal with asking someone else if you can watch a particular show on a particular day. The choices you make and various situations have a positive effect on your psychological well-being.

7. **You will network more**: If you are moving to a new area, you will want to know who your neighbors are, and you will want them to know who you are. If you are in a gated community, they may have a bridge club that you will want to join, and it will be perfect for you to socialize and end up meeting people who make you laugh more. Laughter is always a good thing. They may even have a walking group that walks around the community for exercise, and this is perfect as you will be outside being active and socializing. Forming these

connections is perfect; if something is wrong, you can reach out to your neighbor, and they can send help quicker than a family member who is further away. Your ability to live independently is essential to your happiness.

ISOLATION IS NOT YOUR FRIEND

Let me start by saying that there are some of you who are socially isolated and are totally unbothered by it. In fact, you prefer it, and it does affect you negatively. You prefer being alone, and no form of loneliness creeps in. However, there are many of you who feel alone, mixed with loneliness, and you end up isolating yourself from others, as at times you do not want to appear as a burden. Social isolation and loneliness are different, but they are cousins. There are many factors that contribute to social isolation. Keep in mind that you are all different, so some of these factors may apply and some will not.

Some factors include:

1. **Physical changes**: You may end up with an injury that has not made you disabled, or it could be sickness.

2. **A major shift in your life**: This could occur due to the death of a spouse. This could result in a limited number of people you have contact with, as it could be that they are tied to your spouse, and this can result in a limit on your activities.

3. **Societal and ecological factors**: You could be going through financial difficulties, and in some cases, you

are dealing with poverty. You could have moved somewhere where the transportation system is not that great. This can really kick your social isolation into high gear.

4. **The truth is that social isolation can arise from paramount events**: It could be a combination of minor events that were not dealt with, and they end up growing into something major. Now, how these occurrences impact your life depends on a variety of things, such as the financial, individual, material, and societal resources that you have readily available to you in assisting with coping with these various events that occur. I want you to keep in mind that you are older and have a lot of experience. This can be a key asset in dealing with difficult situations that arise as you get older. However, there are times when things happen in a series, almost like a domino effect. This is where you need to reach out for assistance in dealing with these issues, as it may be just too much for you to deal with. You are not a robot; you are a human being. Nothing is wrong with asking for help.

Ways to Kick Isolation Out the Door

Isolation can almost be deemed the boogeyman, and the boogeyman does have a weakness, and that is light! Bring light into your life and get rid of social isolation, boogeyman. Things to keep in mind to kick isolation right out the door:

1. Maintaining good psychological and physiological health. Stimulate your mind and your body. It will do wonders for your mood and soul.

2. Make sure you save for your retirement years and can afford safe housing or be able to maintain the house you reside in.

3. Being social with your neighbors and keeping active.

4. If possible, choose a gated community to reside in because the safety aspect is better, and that feeling of safety will make you feel better.

5. Make sure that you have healthy relationships with people. Toxicity breeds chaos.

6. Have a great support group. This could be a combination of friends, family, and people in your community.

7. Ensure that you have adequate access to health care and various community services.

8. Ensure that the area where you reside has a great transportation system.

9. Keep challenging yourself and learning something new.

KEEP YOU AND YOUR CASTLE SAFE

Your home is your castle; regardless of its size, it is your sanctuary. Don't let anyone tell you otherwise. There are things that I want you all to keep in mind to keep you and your castle safe and protected:

1. **Checkout tripping hazards**: Make sure that paths around your bed are clutter-free. If the carpet is rising a bit, consider either removing it or taping it down. Keep shoes stored in a safe space, like under your bed

or on a shoe rack, as long as they are out of your way. You should not be stepping over any shoes or stepping on them. Keep your clothes in the hamper; do not place dirty clothes on the floor; you can slip and fall on them.

2. **Do balance exercises**: This minimizes trips and helps you regain your balance quickly if you trip, so you won't hit the floor.

3. **Install rails**: Rails are great for assisting you at various points in your house. Consider a bed rail to help get out of bed or into bed. Install rails by the shower to maintain your balance getting in and out of the shower.

4. **Make sure that you have a fire escape plan**: Anything can happen in your home, and you want to be prepared beforehand so that you do not end up panicking and not knowing what to do. Please ensure that your doors are not blocked in your home. Firefighters have to be able to get into your home in the event that you need to be rescued, and you need to be able to leave safely. Ensure that your fire alarms are working and are loud enough for you to hear. Even if you have a fire extinguisher, in the event of a fire, my advice is: Do not try to put it out yourself; please exit.

5. **Install safety cameras and have adequate lighting on your property**: The world is a crazy place, and unfortunately, there are just some really bad people out there. Having cameras so that you can see who is at your door is a good thing to do. Ensure that you have a panic button so that authorities can reach your property quickly in the event that you cannot make a phone call. You

should always keep your valuables stored safely. Also, do not tell anyone where you stored them.

6. **Keep bath mats in the bathtub**: Having bath mats in the bathtub reduces your chances of slipping while you shower.

7. **Keep all medicines in their original container**: This will prevent you from mixing medicines, which is very dangerous and can cause you harm.

YOU ARE WHAT YOU EAT

I want you all to love what you eat and stay healthy. Nutrition is about the big B. No, I am not talking about your buttocks; I am talking about balance. Having a balanced diet allows your body to get what it needs and is a key component of longevity. When you eat, ensure that you are getting a balanced combination of carbohydrates, fats, proteins, vitamins, minerals, and water. Your body will give you a curtsy as it will be grateful for the nutrients and the necessary elements needed to grow and function properly. Having good nutrition applies to everyone regardless of age, but seeing that I am focusing on the lives of amazing seniors, I have to point out that having good nutrition is very important as it will give you extra energy and help with weight control. Also, remember that having good nutrition can help with certain diseases, such as:

- osteoporosis
- high blood pressure
- heart disease

- type 2 diabetes
- certain cancers

Also, another thing I want you all to remember is that your body and lifestyle have changed as you have gotten older. Okay, maybe you did not need that reminder. But there are certain things in regard to food choices that need to change. You do not need that many calories, but you will still need an ample amount of nutrients. There are some of you who may require more protein in your diet.

Challenges You Can Face With Getting Older and Eating Healthier

You may find it more challenging to eat healthy as you get older due to particular changes. These include:

1. **Living alone**: Now, do not think I am bashing living alone; I am not, and this whole book is all about finding solace in living alone. However, you may not have that same motivation to get up and cook as much and have gotten comfortable ordering out. Nothing is wrong with ordering out, but you are ordering a lot of junk food. For some of you living alone, it could just be that you have a hard time getting around, so even if you want to cook, it is difficult for you. This is where looking into food services that have healthy choices comes in, as they can deliver and save you the hassle, and you will still be keeping up with being healthy.

2. **The medication you are taking**: Many of you are taking different medications for different things, and they

all serve an important purpose. And there are some medications that have certain side effects; there are some that take away your appetite and some that open up your appetite. Speak to your healthcare provider if you find that this is not allowing you to function normally and is robbing you of eating well.

3. **Finances**: Due to certain financial constraints, you lack the capability of purchasing food as often as you would like or are not able to afford healthy foods due to how pricey they are. Find ways to seek assistance that can help you here, whether it is a food voucher or government assistance.

Foods to Eat to Stay Healthy as You Get Older

1. **Stick to foods that are packed with nutrients without too many calories**: Such foods include:

   - Fruits and veggies.
   - Whole grains such as oatmeal, bread made from whole wheat, and brown rice.
   - Milk and cheese with no or very little fat, or milk made from soy or rice with added vitamin D and calcium.
   - Seafood, lean meats, poultry, and eggs
   - Beans, nuts, and seeds

2. **Stay clear of empty calories**: These are the foods that are super tempting, but they are not good for you, and they are packed with calories and very little nutrition. These include:

- ◆ chips

- ◆ soda

- ◆ alcohol

3. **Choose foods that have little cholesterol and fat**: Try to stay away from trans and saturated fats. Animal fats tend to have a lot of saturated fats. Margarine and vegetable shortening are laced with processed fats. When you go to restaurants or fast-food establishments, be mindful that they use fried and baked items.

4. **Good quality H2o**: Water is your best friend! Drink enough liquids, especially water, to avoid dehydration. Due to the medication that some of you take, it is important that you consume a lot of water. Also, I should note that some people lose their thirst and energy. So, unbeknownst to them, they are heading down the dehydration road. So please remember to consume fluids. Set reminders on your phone to drink water.

5. **Try being more active**: If you notice a decline in your appetite, get active. If you are not active, it.

QUICK TIPS IF YOU ARE HAVING TROUBLE EATING HEALTHY

Some of you genuinely want to eat well, but there might be occasional challenges due to your health or other factors. These tips may be helpful:

1. If you are just tired of eating meals by yourself, consider planning some potlucks or cooking with a friend or

family. Also, consider eating at a community center if there is one near you if you are in a gated community and they have one, or at your place of worship.

2. Visit your dentist to ensure that everything is fine if you are experiencing difficulty chewing.

3. Consume a lot of water with your meals if you are experiencing problems swallowing. Consult your healthcare provider if you find that doesn't work. The issue could be brought on by a medical condition or medication you are taking.

4. Make your meal more interesting and festive by adding color and texture if you have difficulties tasting and smelling it.

5. Go the healthy snack route. Add some nutritious snacks to your diet if you find that you aren't eating enough to help you acquire additional calories and nutrients.

6. Consult your doctor if you are having trouble feeding yourself or cooking because of a medical condition. They can suggest an occupational therapist who can assist you in coming up with solutions to make your life easier and simpler.

SAVE FOR A RAINY DAY

When you are prepared for a rainy day, you will find that you will not panic or have high levels of stress. When you are approaching retirement, it is essential to keep a watchful eye on your finances. Now, no size fits all; there are various circumstances that each of you faces. With that said, it is important to construct financial strategies that fit your situation. Keep these tips in mind to assist you when making plans for the future:

1. Ensure you have a pension plan. Sometimes, many people wait until it is too late and end up with no pension plan. Here are a few quick tips you can follow:

- Evaluate how much money you are spending each month by looking at your bank and credit card statements. I know that some of you are still cringing when you read this, but it is something you need to do. Consider how this could be different when you're not doing your job. You will find that you will spend less money when you do not have to travel to work.

- Determine how much money you will receive each month after you retire. This includes funds acquired upon retirement, earnings obtained from bank deposits, investments in companies, or the act of saving money. Go through everything with a fine toothcomb. Also, explore the advantages and benefits that will be available to you after you retire.

- Pick a retirement date and a date when your state pension will be paid. Having a specific date will allow you to plan better and be more prepared.

- Find out what you are entitled to and how it will be paid to you by contacting your current and previous pension providers. It is all about being prepared and knowing everything; in doing so, it will help you set realistic financial goals.

2. If you want to stay on the proper path, save your money and avoid feelings of wrath. See what I did there? It's catchy, isn't it? The truth is, no one wants to pay bills. I do not know one person who pays any bills with a smile on their face. But it is essential to take care of our bills so that we can live. There is no escaping the light bill, rent or mortgage payment, supermarket, and pharmacy expenses; we simply cannot avoid them. Please keep these essential bills in mind when you are planning for your future. You will have less income after retirement, so factor these into your budget.

3. Consider investments. By investing, you have the potential to generate consistent earnings or accrue a significant nest egg for your post-work life. This can help with calming your mind, and a calm mind equals stress and clarity.

4. Organize your power of attorney and ensure that your will is written. I know this can seem so final. However, this is something that you all should do. It avoids confusion when you transition, especially if you have children. It is very important that you also look into getting your power of attorney in order. It is a legal document that gives a representative, who is chosen by you, authority to make decisions on your behalf if, for whatever reason, you are no longer able to do so. Quick lesson: There are different types of power of attorney:

- A regular power of attorney holds validity only until you temporarily lose the capacity to think and make certain decisions on your own. This is super helpful if you need someone to help you for a short time. Let's say you went through surgery and will be in the hospital for a certain period of time, or if you need someone to handle your bank accounts for you, then an ordinary power of attorney is the right choice. Please be careful when selecting your regular power of attorney, especially when it comes to your finances. Take your time selecting one.

- A lasting power of attorney (LPA) is divided into two categories: One is for making choices about money, and the other is for making choices about personal care. When you create an LPA for financial choices, you can choose whether to allow your representative to use it when you are still mentally capable or not. Otherwise, this will only happen when you are no longer able to think or understand things properly (Josh, 2023). This is why it is imperative to get these in order beforehand; you have to be prepared, and life is very unpredictable.

5. Get your will in order. I am not trying to make any of you freak out; however, too many times, people do deal with these things, and many people end up in family feuds or the wrong person ends up with things they should not have received. It is important that you get your will dealt with. This is something that every adult should think about, not just seniors; death can come at different times, and it is not limited to people who are elders. If you have kids or other people who rely on you. Your will is a document that says what should happen to your money and other things when you pass. Many people delay creating a will because it is a topic that makes them uncomfortable. Please note that I am

not trying to make any one of you uncomfortable; I just want you all to be prepared. However, if you die without a will, your belongings will be controlled by the rules of intestacy. This means that if you don't make plans for what happens to your things after you die, the government will decide instead, and they might not give them to the people you choose. For instance, only married couples, registered partners, and a few other close family members can receive an inheritance according to these rules. Tips to keep in mind when making a will:

- Get advice from a lawyer who is an expert in that specific area of law. Doing so will give you the proper guidelines you need.

- Make sure to include everything you want distributed or shared after you transition; this includes things like houses or other properties, money saved, money put into investments, and personal belongings.

- Clearly explain how you want your belongings and property to be shared among your loved ones, friends, or charities after you pass away.

- Choose someone or more than one person to take care of your estate when you pass away. They will ensure that what you ask for gets done. They will also handle the payment of inheritance tax if it is necessary.

6. Include funeral costs when budgeting your money after retirement. I promise I am not trying to be Debbie Downer. I know that talking about funerals can make people feel uneasy and sad. But in actuality, they are

also really expensive and can cause a lot of stress for your family after your passing. The price of funerals has been going up consistently for a few years. It is best to have that money put aside along with how you would like your funeral proceedings to go; this will eliminate any form of confusion or conflict after your passing.

NEVER STOP WATERING YOUR TREE OF KNOWLEDGE AND GROWTH

The seeds that you have planted in yourself since you were younger have all grown into various trees. Some of you have one tree with various branches that each have different types of fruit. Your tree is unique to you. What I want all of you to never forget is that you are never too old to learn anything. Your mind is very powerful and always wants to grow. Some of you, over time, have forgotten this, and your trees are thirsty and just need you to water them. Remember, wise ones, that there are more than simply tangible advantages to learning. It also plays a huge role in promoting your general happiness and mental wellness.

Here are some reminders as to why you should never stop watering your trees of knowledge and growth:

1. **The more you learn, the more memory improves**: I hope this is something you keep in mind and never forget. As many of you know, the older you get, the harder it becomes for you to remember things. Sometimes, you find it difficult to navigate the area you live in or remember what exactly you planned on purchas-

ing at the supermarket or market. Let me just quickly say that this is something that can happen to anyone. That is why I am a firm believer in writing lists. However, I digress; you get the point. Sometimes, you can forget things that are very important to you. It's similar to losing a part of who you are. This feeling can feed negative thoughts in your head, and before you know it, you start overthinking and begin to think that it is not too late for you to learn anything. Well, I am here to remind you all that this is not true! However, you can avoid that by keeping your mind busy. Doing any kind of activity that exercises your brain is better than doing nothing at all. However, the most effective way to keep your memory sharp is by learning new things or mastering a new skill.

2. **It makes you feel like you achieved something**: I don't know about you, but there is nothing that feels better than getting a better version of the phone I had or upgrading my computer. It performs better; it's quicker! Exciting! Gaining new knowledge is similar to that. You do better at your daily tasks, understand things better, and get along with the people and things around you easier. This will make you feel more sure of yourself and increase your sense of achievement. Everyone loves that feeling of accomplishment! It doesn't matter what you decide to learn. It could be a new thing you can do with technology, or you might want to learn the most used words in French for when you go to French-speaking countries. No matter what it is, learning new things will make you a better person and give you a sense of pride.

3. **You will discover something new about yourself**: Although it sounds like a cliché, it's true that you will never know unless you try. Sometimes, you place doubt on yourself without even attempting the activity. You can enroll in dance classes for pleasure or attempt to study a foreign language out of sheer interest and discover that you have a natural talent for these things. You will learn about the interests and activities that make you happy and content through the process of trying new things and increasing your knowledge.

4. **It helps you develop self-confidence**: Self-confidence is an important aspect of happiness, and happiness is something you all deserve. Let me share something with you: There are some people who become more confident the older they get, while others lose their confidence easily because their situation keeps changing. As you get older, your bodies and minds naturally change. There are those of you who embrace the change, while there are some of you for whom the physical change really messes with you on a mental level. This can sometimes cause you to forget who you really are or to feel unhappy when you take a glance in the mirror. When you learn something new, it helps you feel more positive about who you are. In simpler words, it means that if you dedicate time and work hard, you can make progress in anything.

5. **Continuously learning helps you stay up-to-date**: Have you ever been around your children or grandchildren, or maybe been at a park and heard young people and had no idea what they were talking about? When you get into learning more and constantly seeking knowledge, it will help you stay updated and

understand new trends and various things that are happening on a technological level. You may not have the same interests and hobbies as children, grandchildren, or the young people in the community, but making an effort to keep up with their world will make the time you spend together more enjoyable for both of you. Simply put, it won't feel as if you are living in completely separate realities.

6. **It makes your social life better**: As time goes by, the number of people we interact with decreases. Do you remember when you were in high school? It was like you made new friends almost every week and ended up with this large group of friends. In college, your friend circle was smaller. These tend to be the ones that we have into adulthood, and then when you become working members of society, you do not plan on making any friends at work, but you end up forming a bond with someone, and it sticks. Now that you are at this stage in your life, it is good to still be social and interactive. Taking a class in a different language, like yoga, origami, or something you enjoy, is a wonderful chance to make friends with people who like the same things as you.

TIPS ON HOW TO CHALLENGE YOURSELF AND KEEP LEARNING

1. **Get into yoga and meditation**: This will do wonders for your body and your mind. There are a ton of instructional videos on YouTube that can help you. However, to avoid straining a muscle or really harming yourself,

it might be helpful to take some lessons with an instructor. Also, this could be a chance to meet people who have similar interests.

2. **Become proficient in a language from another country**: I keep bringing this up because it is great learning a new language, and you will love the feeling you have when you have mastered it! Choose a particular language that you have always wanted to learn about, or pick one that will be useful to you for your future trips.

3. **Get up and go dancing**: Being active is important for your body, but exercise doesn't have to be difficult. There are dances that anyone of any age and physical ability can do. Maybe you want to learn to do the salsa, but your age does not limit you from learning to swing those hips a little.

4. **Why not give gardening a try?** The tranquility that you get from gardening is indescribable! You will spend more time outside, and you can eat the food you grow.

5. **You can think about giving painting or photography a try**: It's a good way to be aware of what's happening around you and develop your creative side. You will notice how more observant and appreciative of nature you are.

6. **Listen, no matter what you choose, learning something new will make you wiser and help you in a variety of ways**. That will leave you fulfilled and make your spirit leap for you. Think about it: Maybe there is something you wanted to learn for a long time but never had the chance. Well, now is your chance to make that leap!

Share Your Wisdom With Others

Dear wise ones, it is important that your wisdom tree, which is filled with fruits of knowledge and wisdom, be something you share with others. I understand that some of you may be apprehensive about doing this because some younger people do not treat older people well and are rude to them. They think that older people are not useful anymore, have nothing valuable to offer, and don't deserve much respect. I think this perspective is strange, and these young people will eventually grow older. Anyway, I find this method of thinking a huge mistake. As all of you know, you are wise beyond your years. Because you all have lived for a long time, you have a lot of knowledge and experience that we can all benefit from.

Wisdom flows from experience. The things you have gone through in your life and the knowledge you have gained from them are really helpful and good for people who are younger than you. Be brave and look for chances to tell others about it. You can volunteer at a club or shelter and use it as a way to share what you know and offer guidance. All of you have been through different situations that impact people's lives nowadays. Older adults who have gone through similar experiences can offer valuable advice and support to younger people in areas like work, school, or the military. You can teach them how to deal with certain situations, and it can assist them in making specific choices in their lives. You have an understanding of how to interact with people on a personal level. There might be someone in your neighborhood or where you are helping out who is having trouble with a family member or friend or is unsure about what to expect from being married. Teaching that person what you know will really help because you can understand and tell them about your own experiences. You will be able to help people with their problems and answer their questions more easily. Life today can be very overwhelming and filled with pressure. Although there are major problems happening globally, our daily lives can also be filled with stress. Some of you have experienced wars, recessions, and other hard times. Sharing your experiences and advice with others can help you see the world and your own life more clearly.

You have a healthy approach to life. The things you can teach others are not just about getting through tough times. A lot of you have lived for a long time and are relatively healthy. Many people can learn from you how to have a good time in their lives. Some of you like to have fun and relax during the day, and you know how to go with the flow. Older people understand that not all issues are extremely terrible. You are good at handling problems, and you always try to find something good in almost every situation. You know that one key to health and happiness is to keep a positive outlook. A lot of you are surprised by how seriously some young people approach life. This can disrupt their ability to enjoy themselves and take a break to relax. This can also be why there are some younger people who cannot handle pressure well and tend to be very irritated because they do not know when to take a chill pill. Your knowledge will be very useful to a lot of people in these situations.

Share your senior wisdom with someone today; do not have the "when they get older, they will find out for themselves" approach. Tell them that there is a better way to do things, which can prevent certain problems and issues from arising in their lives. You can impart some of your life experiences to young people and other people in general and let them learn from your knowledge and wisdom.

Volunteer at a community center where you can engage with younger people. It can go far. You are very wise, and your wisdom is extremely valuable. Discover a method to communicate and engage with others, as it will improve and enhance your life. You will be sharing knowledge that they cannot learn from books. It can be a great relationship that is good for both you and the other person.

DEAR WISE ONES

Dear wise ones, I need to leave these thoughts with you. I want to remind you that you are important because you have special qualities that make you unique. People like you for being yourself, including your appearance and the way you speak. All the things you really enjoy doing as hobbies make people even more interested in you. It helps them reach out to you and allows you to reach out to them. Never forget that you are special and different from others. This is an important thing to remember in life. Never, ever forget that. This should be the thing that keeps you going in life. Your special qualities are very valuable and cannot be replaced, whether it's the wrinkles on your face, the way your eyes get bright when you laugh, your gray hair, the jokes you make, or the music you enjoy. You have an amazing and beautiful way of expressing yourself. Welcome and accept this phase of your life, and you will notice that many people will be drawn to you. What you think is normal about you is actually exceptional.

There are people that you have helped that you did not even know you helped by simply telling them good morning with a smile. What you expressed might have served as the catalyst for someone to do something that positively impacted their situation. Doing something nice for someone could have made them feel better mentally. A message you posted on social media may have made everyone who read it laugh. The emotions that you shared with someone else might have helped them see life differently. You are smart. Your story of when you were in school and stood up to a bully may inspire someone to stand up for themselves or take action. Your generosity in sharing resources with a friend in need could improve their circumstances. Your children or grandchildren, or even the children in the community, might look up to you because of how you treated them when they were feeling down or alone.

Maybe someone close to you has told you that you are strong and can handle anything because you have already faced and overcome difficult challenges in the past. You know what you are good at. But the most important thing is that you are the kind of person who can overcome difficulties and keep going no matter what. You always know how to handle difficult situations when the timing is right. Always remember to be kind to yourself. Always remember that you have the ability to achieve anything, and there is nothing that can stop you. When you think about your life, you can feel happy because you always persevered and never gave up. You faced and overcame every difficult situation. No one else can make others as happy as you can. And you don't even realize it because being kind, understanding, and compassionate comes naturally to you. You make it a habit to make other people happy. There are so many people who get happy when they receive text messages from you. They feel happy when you tell them that you remember them. People are excited and happy to be with you or receive a call from you. Sometimes, just being there for someone can make them really happy and brighten their day. I hope that these words resonate with you, keep you in the present, and truly appreciate just how much your tree of wisdom and knowledge has and can impact the lives of many.

You have discovered the art of living alone, embracing independence, health, financial savvy, safety, community, growth, longevity, and wisdom. Now, take these tools and paint your own unique picture of a joyful, independent life. Your journey does not end here; it is just beginning. It is a new and exciting chapter that you are embarking on, and you will be great at it; nothing can stop you! Embrace the insights and strategies you have learned, and continue to shape a fulfilling, fearless life on your own terms.

CHAPTER
"GOOD WILL"

Helping others without expectation of anything in return has been proven to lead to increased happiness and satisfaction in life.

I would love to give you the chance to experience that same feeling during your reading or listening experience today...

All it takes is a few moments of your time to answer one simple question:

Would you make a difference in the life of someone you've never met—without spending any money or seeking recognition for your good will?

If so, I have a small request for you.

If you've found value in your reading or listening experience today, I humbly ask that you take a brief moment right now to leave an honest review of this book. It won't cost you anything but 30 seconds of your time—just a few seconds to share your thoughts with others.

Your voice can go a long way in helping someone else find the same inspiration and knowledge that you have.

Are you familiar with leaving a review for an Audible, Kindle, or e-reader book? If so, it's simple:

If you're on **Audible**: just hit the three dots in the top right of your device, click rate & review, then leave a few sentences about the book along with your star rating.

If you're reading on **Kindle** or an e-reader, simply scroll to the last page of the book and swipe up—the review should prompt from there.

If you're on a **Paperback** or any other physical format of this book, you can find the book page on Amazon (or wherever you bought this) and leave your review right there.

REFERENCES

A quote by John (n.d.). Dome. https://web.cs.dal.ca/~johnston/poetry/island.html

All of the benefits of elderly living at home. (2019, August 6). Carelink. https://www.carelink.org/all-of-the-benefits-of-elderly-living-at-home/

Atherton, H. (2023). *The secret to resilience is consistency and self-reflection*. Hacia Atherton. https://haciaatherton.com/the-secret-to-resilience-is-consistency-and-self-reflection/

Ausubel, J. (2020, March 10). *Older people are more likely to live alone in the U.S. than elsewhere in the world*. Pew Research Center. https://www.pewresearch.org/short-reads/2020/03/10/older-people-are-more-likely-to-live-alone-in-the-u-s-than-elsewhere-in-the-world/

Ball, J. (2022, November 22). *I'm a dietitian who just started living alone—here's what I've learned about cooking for one*. Eating Well. https://www.eatingwell.com/article/7828600/dietitian-living-alone-cooking-for-one/

Borwick, K. (2023, August 14). *How to make a budget for retirement. Annuity.org.* https://www.annuity.org/retirement/planning/retirement-budget/

Brennan, B. MD. (2021, October 25). *What to know about living alone after 60. WebMD.* https://www.webmd.com/healthy-aging/what-to-know-about-living-alone-after-60

Flicker, J., Carreau, G. (2023, August 17). *How to learn new things. WikiHow.* https://www.wikihow.com/Learn-New-Things

Fontana, L., Partridge, L., Longo, V.D. (2010, April 16). *Extending healthy life span--from yeast to humans. National Library of Medicine.* https://pubmed.ncbi.nlm.nih.gov/20395504/

4 habits of "superagers". (2023). *Northwestern Medicine.* https://www.nm.org/healthbeat/healthy-tips/4-habits-super-agers

80% of older Americans cannot pay for long-term care or withstand a financial shock, new study shows. (2023, April 19). *NCO.* https://www.ncoa.org/article/80-percent-of-older-americans-cannot-pay-for-long-term-care-or-withstand-a-financial-shock-new-study-shows

Geier, B. (2023, March 18). *Being Smart Asset.* https://smartasset.com/retirement/how-to-invest-for-retirement-50

Gormandy-White, M. (2022, September 21). *44 Being alone quotes to embrace your solitude. Love to Know.* https://www.lovetoknow.com/quotes-quips/daily-life/being-alone-quotes

Griffin, R.M. (2021, November 4). *Turmeric (Curcumin). Web-MD.* https://www.webmd.com/diet/supplement-guide-turmeric#:~:text=Curcumin%2C%20a%20substance%20in%20turmeric,turmeric%20might%20also%20be%20medicinal.

Haralalka, R. (2017, December 13). *6 clever ways to make your home elderly-friendly. Houzz.* https://www.houzz.in/magazine/6-clever-ways-to-make-your-home-elderly-friendly-stsetivw-vs~96809400

Huldie, J. (2023). *The impact of past life experiences on current life situations. This Mom's Confession.* https://www.janinehuldie.com/the-impact-of-past-life-experiences-on-current-life-situations/

Josh. (2023, July 12). *Top 10 finance tips for older people. Life Connect 24.* https://www.lifeconnect24.co.uk/blog/top-10-finance-tips-for-older-people/

Kaminski, S. (2022, March 11). *Why you should never stop learning new things. Red Hot Mamas.* https://redhotmamas.org/why-you-should-never-stop-learning-new-things/

Kilroy, D.S. (2023, March 27). *Exercise plan for seniors. Heathline.* https://www.healthline.com/health/everyday-fitness/senior-workouts

Loneliness and social isolation — tips for staying connected. (2021, January 14). *NIH.* https://www.nia.nih.gov/health/loneliness-and-social-isolation-tips-staying-connected#:~:text=Being%20alone%20may%20leave%20older,%2C%20depression%2C%20and%20cognitive%20decline.

Markway, B. PhD. (2018, September 20). *Why self-confidence is more important than you think. Psychology Today.* https://www.psychologytoday.com/intl/blog/shyness-is-nice/201809/why-self-confidence-is-more-important-you-think

Nutrition as we age: healthy eating with the dietary guidelines. (2021, July 20). *Health. gov.* https://health.gov/news/202107/nutrition-we-age-healthy-eating-dietary-guidelines

Nutrition for older adults. (2019, May 30). *Medline Plus.* https://medlineplus.gov/nutritionforolderadults.html

Nuts and your heart: Eating nuts for heart health. (2022, April 2). *Mayo Clinic.* https://www.mayoclinic.org/diseases-conditions/heart-disease/in-depth/nuts/art-20046635#:~:text=Nuts%20are%20a%20good%20source,fats%20%E2%80%94%20lower%20bad%20cholesterol%20levels.

Pardue- Spears, C. (2022, March 14). *4 benefits of lifelong learning for seniors & older adults. Family Matters.* https://familymattershc.com/benefits-of-lifelong-learning-for-seniors/#:~:text=Ongoing%20learning%20helps%20sharpen%20cognitive,for%20aging%20men%20and%20women

Past experiences — how they shape us. (2023). *Peaceful Soul.* https://peacefulsoul.co/the-mind/past-experiences/

Petre, A. (2023, March 16). *Habits to form now for a longer life. Healthline.* https://www.healthline.com/nutrition/13-habits-linked-to-a-long-life

Reasons independence is important for seniors. (2021, March 5). *Vantage.* https://vantageaging.org/blog/independence-is-important-for-seniors/#:~:text=Independence%20gives%20seniors%20a%20sense,even%20if%20they%20seem%20small.

Respecting seniors and their wisdom. (2023). *Miami Home Care Services.* https://miamihomecareservices.com/blog/respecting-seniors-and-their-wisdom/

Rogalski, E. PhD. (2017). *What makes someone a SuperAger? Northwestern Medicine.* https://www.feinberg.northwestern.edu/research/podcast/what-makes-someone-a-superager.html

Sharpe, R. (2021, December 4). *You are important: 12 reasons why you matter. Declutter the Mind.* https://declutterthemind.com/blog/you-are-important/

Social isolation of seniors - Volume 1: Understanding the issue and finding solutions. (2021, April 14). *Government of Canada.* https://www.canada.ca/en/employment-social-development/corporate/partners/seniors-forum/social-isolation-toolkit-vol1.html

Success over 50: Top 10 career success stories. (2021, August 7). Careline365. https://www.careline.co.uk/success-top-10-late-bloomers/

7 tips to help you in your decision-making process. (n.d.). Psych Central. https://psychcentral.com/health/tips-to-help-you-make-the-most-important-decisions

6 self-esteem-boosting activities for aging adults. (2019, April 23). Home Care Assistance. https://www.homecareassistanceroseville.com/activities-that-boost-self-esteem-in-elderly

The benefits of meal prep for seniors. (2019, March 25). Companion for Seniors. https://companionsforseniors.com/2019/03/benefits-meal-prep-planning-seniors/

The importance of self-reflection as you age in a senior living home in Indialantic, FL. (2023). Discovery Village. https://www.discoveryvillages.com/senior-living-blog/the-importance-of-self-reflection-as-you-age-in-a-senior-living-home-in-indialantic-fl/

Robinson, L. (2023, February 28). *The mental health benefits of exercise. Help Guide. Org.* https://www.helpguide.org/articles/healthy-living/the-mental-health-benefits-of-exercise.htm

The science of longevity. (2017). Clinique La Prairie. https://cliniquelaprairie.com/en/science-longevity

Tip sheet: home safety tips for older adults. (2019, June). Health Aging. https://www.healthinaging.org/tools-and-tips/tip-sheet-home-safety-tips-older-adults

14 exercises for seniors to improve strength and balance. (2023). Lifeline. https://www.lifeline.ca/en/resources/14-exercises-for-seniors-to-improve-strength-and-balance/

West, T.C. (2023, May 25). *Six key housing factors to consider as you age.* Kiplinger. https://www.kiplinger.com/retirement/housing-factors-to-consider-as-you-age

Why hobbies are important. (2023). *Skilled at Life.* https://www.skilledatlife.com/why-hobbies-are-important/

Wooll, M. (2022, June 7). *It's time for a fresh start: How to embrace new beginnings at 50. BetterUp.* https://www.betterup.com/blog/how-to-start-over-in-life-at-50

ABOUT THE AUTHOR

This author has a knack for capturing the essence of life's complexities, intricacies, and universal truths through her writing, often presenting thought-provoking perspectives on various aspects of existence. Her life books are characterized by rich character development, as the author skillfully weaves together the stories of diverse topics, illuminating journeys, challenges, and triumphs. Through books, the author explores themes such as love, passion, victory, identity, personal growth, and the search for meaning, offering readers profound insights and moments of introspection.

Beyond Zoë's professional accomplishments, she also has a rich and multifaceted life outside of publishing. This book is a testament to her commitment to providing valuable insights and practical guidance. The author's books are often praised for their ability to evoke empathy in readers, fostering a deep connection between the readers and the valuable insights they encounter within the pages.

The author is a distinguished authority in various fields of study, bringing a wealth of knowledge and experience to her thought-provoking non-fiction works. As you delve into Zoë's manuscripts, you can expect to embark on an intellectual journey guided by Zoë's profound insights and intentional thought-provoking passion for self -development.   Her non-fiction works continue to push the boundaries of knowledge, inviting readers to expand their horizons and gain a deeper understanding of life and its impact on our success.

Zoë's works have been praised for their meticulous research, insightful analysis, and the way they challenge readers to think critically about the world around them.

Any one of Zoë's latest book,....

1. **Unlocking Infinity: Master the Art of Longevity**

   Learn How to, Boost Your Brain Health, Recharge Your Immune System and Restore Youthful Balance in 3 Easy Steps

2. **Living Your Best Life: Radiate from Within**

   Ultimate Guide to Finding Purpose & Fulfillment in 3 Easy Steps.

3. **Alone, But Not Lonely: Aging on Your Terms**

   A Roadmap for Aging Independently, Striking Balance & Finding Purpose

4. **Longevity: The Art of Aging Backwards**

   Step-by-Step Guide to Renew, Restore and Reverse Aging Mentally, Physically & Spiritually

5. **Journeying Alone, Journeying Strong: Navigating Aging Alone Without Children**

   Self-Help Guide to Finding Inner Strength, Peace, Joy & Fulfillment in Childless Aging

6. **Mastering the Steps to Success: Achieving Success at Every Rung**

   Proven Strategies for Overcoming Obstacles and Reaching Greatness. Develop, Learn, Succeed

7. **The Positivity Code: Supercharge Your Life with Positive Thinking**

   Learn The Art of Positive Thinking, Changing Your Life One Thought at a Time

8. **The Growth Mindset Code: Cracking the Secrets to Success**

   Comprehensive Guide to Breaking Limits with A Growth Mindset, Cultivating Unlimited Possibilities

9. **The Superfood Prescription: Refuel Your Mind & Body**

   100 Supercharged Foods to Revitalize & Transform Your Health

... is another testament to her dedication to delivering enlightening and captivating non-fiction literature. Whether you're a seasoned reader of non-fiction or new to the genre Zoë's work is sure to engage, inform, and inspire.

To stay updated on **Zoë Publishing's** latest projects and musings, visit us on **facebook.com/zoepublishing** and follow us on Instagram & Tik Tok **(@zoepublishing)**